MW01026137

Praise for *Turnaround*

"*Turnaround* is a powerful challenge from my friend Senator James Lankford to pay more attention to who we are, rather than just what we do. James' practical leadership ideas will encourage you to live your faith and find impactful ways to serve our community and our great nation. Every chapter is packed with history, humor, and inspiration to be part of our national turnaround."

—MIKE POMPEO, 70th United States Secretary of State, former Congressman, and *New York Times* bestselling author of *Never Give an Inch*

"The best sermons are seen, not just heard. Senator James Lankford lives his faith with humility, grace, collegiality, and authenticity. In this book, he adroitly puts his finger precisely on the key to change and revival in our country. The key is *us*. This book is both a challenge and a chance for us to reflect and act."

—TREY GOWDY, lawyer, former Congressman, #1 *New York Times* bestselling author, and host of FOX's *Sunday Night in America with Trey Gowdy*

"It's encouraging when politicians of any party or group pursue policies that benefit Americans and strengthen families. My friend, Senator James Lankford, is a man of high character and deep Christian commitment. *Turnaround* offers an impactful message that transcends politics and will resonate with every American who values faith, family, and freedom. There's no question America is facing daunting challenges, but those challenges are not insurmountable. I appreciate James' clarion call to recommit ourselves to those foundational values upon which our country was founded and which transcend politics."

—JIM DALY, president and CEO of Focus on the Family
and author of *Finding Home*

"In the cynicism that has taken over the U.S., a common cliche is that all the politicians are out for themselves. No one who knows Senator James Lankford has ever said that. James' folksy stories of finding common ground in the airport with a political opponent or shopping for toilets at Home Depot is the James I know. This book is good old fashioned government, 'by the people.' It's a great and enlightening read. James is at the highest level of leadership in the most powerful country in the world, yet he's truly one of us."

—KEN HARRISON, CEO of WaterStone, former CEO of
Promise Keepers and author of *Rise of the Servant Kings*

TURNAROUND

America's Revival

JAMES LANKFORD

United States Senator

Oklahoma

Humanix Books

www.humanixbooks.com

ISBN: 978-1-63006-290-3 (Hardcover)
ISBN: 978-1-63006-291-0 (E-book)

Printed in the United States of America
10 9 8 7 6 5 4 3 2 1

"Because of the Lord's great love
we are not consumed,
for his compassions never fail.
They are new every morning;
great is your faithfulness."

—LAMENTATIONS 3:22-23 NIV

Contents

Author's Note

I want to be a part of the solution. Without question, so do you, or you wouldn't have opened this book. The most common statement I hear from people is, "Fix it!" These pages are a challenge to myself and my great neighbors to live our values and turn around the course of our nation. We can, but will we?

We are frustrated and angry about the world as we see it, but we are also optimistic about the future. We feel the frustration in our wallet, but we really feel it in our soul; it could and should be better. We know it can be better, much better, but it will take decisions and action from each of us.

This is not a challenge to be angry about our challenges; it is a calling and a plan. It is a realistic view of where we are and an optimistic path out of the mire. I have filled the pages with personal stories, frank questions, spiritual challenges, and a healthy dose of humor. It is my prayer that we catch a glimpse of ourselves in the mirror and fix our national bed head.

I am incredibly grateful on my life's journey to have experienced the grace and forgiveness of Jesus and to walk through life with my bride, Cindy, and our two remarkable daughters,

Hannah and Jordan. They are God's greatest gifts in my life. The best stories in my life circle around them. No matter what task I have in my life, Child of God, Husband, and Daddy are still the titles that matter the most.

Introduction

Every year, for decades, thousands of people from across the political spectrum in the United States are asked a simple question: "Is America on the right track?" For years, Americans have answered overwhelmingly, "No!"

It will take more than an election to get us on the right track. Elections reveal trends, but they don't change us. We still have work to do. After every election, we still must determine what our nation will become tomorrow. Those decisions are not made by the folks in Washington; they are made by each individual "me," who collectively define the "we" of the United States.

Our lives are the result of millions of decisions, including the decision to pick up this book. Our actions today will affect our own future and the future of the nation. That means changing our nation's future and our families starts with deciding whether we are willing to change first, set the example first, speak first, or love first.

I'm a good driver—not flawless, but not bad. No speeding tickets and no big accidents. (ask me another time why I use the words "no big accidents.") Not long ago, I was offered an opportunity from an insurance company to put a tracking device on my car to get cheaper insurance rates. Tracking devices are not my thing, but cheaper rates are music to my ears. So I said yes, for a while.

After the tracking device arrived, I felt like I had just installed an unjust electronic minder in my front right seat with a clipboard scoring every moment of every drive to the office, the store, or the airport (when I was running late). As most people do when they are behind the wheel, I give myself grace and other people judgment. But now I couldn't just score myself with an A; I had to earn an A. I wanted cheaper car insurance rates, but I understood quickly that I had to drive like someone who deserved cheaper rates. For the record, I earned the cheaper rates—and then I got the electronic minder out of my car as fast as possible.

Americans want a better nation, but we often want it for free. We want someone else to serve, someone else to lead, or someone else to set the example. Freedom always has a cost. Always. A moral nation grows from personal responsibility and sacrifice. We cannot grade ourselves with grace and others with judgment; each person must live up to the America we all want to see. No one turns around by accident. You have to make an intentional decision to do life a different way to get a different result.

Our American Constitution protects the right of all people to think, choose, and determine their direction. That noisy pursuit of a more perfect union has dominated us for more than two and a half centuries. After a 250-year road trip, we now find ourselves at the latest crossroads of individual liberty and personal responsibility. We want to do anything, say anything, and watch anything, but we also want everyone else to live right so they don't affect us. In real life, it does not work that way. When I passively sit back, it hurts me, my family, and other people.

This is a journey book. It's not written to be slurped down; it's written to be chewed on like a steak. It's best read with others for discussion, confession, and challenge. Processing together is one of the lost gifts of authentic relationships and growth. We eat together, play together, but often fail to challenge each other to be better. This book will give you the opportunity to challenge yourself and others to determine what happens next in your lives, families, and nation.

Change, especially life-altering change, happens best with others. If you choose to read this book alone, think through it with someone you can talk to about your thoughts and hear their life journey as well. Shifting direction in life is easier with a friend. It could be that you are the first "shifter" in your family or group of friends. You will be the role model for everyone else. If the attitude and actions of friends, family, or community are going to get better, someone must go first. It might as well be you.

Recent books on culture and politics, from all sides of the political spectrum, seem to inspire fear and anger. Certainly, there are plenty of things drastically wrong in our remarkable country. However, this book is not about all our problems; it's about our future and how and when things get better through each of us.

I'm a person who has been transformed by the grace of Jesus, and I'm an unapologetically conservative American. But this book welcomes people from every perspective into a dialogue about our individual responsibility, our challenges, and our nation's future. I interact with people every day who disagree with my point of view, but I hear them out because I know I still have more to learn in life.

Changing the future for those in poverty is hard. Saying, "I was wrong. Will you forgive me?" is hard. Elevating a culture is hard. Loving someone who does not care about you is hard. Being a role model is hard. Solving the border crisis, paying down the national debt, and limiting the overreaching power of government are all hard—I know that firsthand. They're all hard, but I bet you would agree that it's past time to do hard things. Just because something is hard doesn't mean it can't be done or shouldn't be done.

Our national challenges of debt, lawlessness, and moral drift are overwhelming. However, we can realistically and joyfully confront our situation and together solve our biggest challenges. Working is so much better than whining. Praying is so much better than complaining. Lifting up is so much better than tearing down.

Right now, someone in America is selling drugs, and someone else is walking a friend through addiction recovery. Someone is dropping out of school, and someone is mentoring a child. Someone is yelling at their neighbor, and someone is taking their kids to the park to play with new friends. The difference between each of these contrasting examples was thousands of individual decisions and influences. You can choose the first step today to intentionally start your family and your nation down a better road. Your choice today will determine the future of America tomorrow.

1

WHAT WE SEE IN THE MIRROR

"As water reflects the face,
so one's life reflects the heart."

—PROVERBS 27:19

As a child, I was told if you break a mirror, it's bad luck. I really don't know why. I always assumed it was because mirrors were expensive, and if you broke it, Mom would help you understand how expensive they were. That's definitely bad luck.

People put mirrors in bathrooms, hallways, dining rooms, closets, offices, and elevators. We put mirrors in rooms to make them look larger, mirrors on our car that make things look smaller, mirrored windows on the outside of office towers, close-up mirrors in a bathroom, and full-length mirrors to see how our shoes work with the outfit (though for me, shoes are just shoes). Mirrors aren't new, but they are useful. The Met in New York City has ancient Egyptian mirrors on display from 3,500 years ago. Apparently, humanity has always tried to see and fix that one hair standing straight up. I can only imagine the consequence of breaking a 3,500-year-old mirror—that would be some seriously bad luck.

The mirror in my bathroom gets the terrible daily duty of reflecting my epic bed head every morning. Each day, I am convinced that I looked better when I went to bed the night before than I do each morning. My hair looks like a battle raged all night between the forces of good and evil and the evil forces won.

Mirrors don't create; they just reflect. If you don't like what you see in the mirror, you have options: You can deny it and walk away; threaten or intimidate the mirror until it improves your image; or acknowledge what you see in the mirror is accurate and change is needed. You can shout at the mirror or accuse it of reflecting someone else, but it doesn't change the reality of the reflection in the mirror. That's still my bed head looking back at me, in serious need of some work.

We look at our bed head each day, not because we need an early-morning shock, but because we are convinced with a little work, it could be presentable in public (a good thing for everyone). We look in the mirror because we have a hopeful action plan for our head to look better in the future than it does now.

When some people watch the news, they have the same reaction I have to seeing myself in the mirror each morning: "What a mess! What happened to our government, our culture and our patriotism? How did that happen while I was sleeping?" We see rising crime, growing national debt, an exploding cost of living, broken families, kids who can't read, and distracted parents. We have elections in our country to send people to fix the mess we see in Washington but we also need hopeful and committed Americans who will say, "This can get better with a little work, starting right now, with me."

THE BIG MIRROR

The public conflicts of Washington spring from the private arguments in our families, social media, and workplaces more than we want to admit. Thanksgiving is a good test case. If your extended family gets together at Thanksgiving, good for you. People often tell me they cut their holiday travel because too many arguments broke out last time the extended family got together. Last Thanksgiving, some family member decided to

wear an environmentally friendly, gender-neutral, animal-test-
ing-free, defund-the-police T-shirt just to bug an open-carry,
closed-border, talk-show-addicted, capitalist cousin. Arguments
broke out over dinner, and the picture-perfect family meal dis-
integrated into hot yelling, cold silence, or meaningless small
talk. The conversation on the ride home was memorable though.

If this sounds familiar, then realize it's not just D.C.
that's divided; it's us, too. Contrary to the belief of some that
Washington is an anomaly, a weird swampy freak show that is
drastically different from the rest of the country, Washington is
just a mirror to the nation.

Those who think about politics all the time—you know who
you are—sometimes forget that elections are only one aspect of
our national direction. Elections don't change who we are; elections *reveal* who we are. An election gives a quick look into the
mind and emotion of our nation at that moment. Long before
the election, each citizen had a story that affected how they
voted or even whether they voted. The final vote tally is just one
page of our national story.

That doesn't mean you shouldn't vote or be involved in the
future of our Republic; you absolutely should. Please research
and vote in every election. Just don't think that all the country
needs right now is the perfect election
and suddenly everything is solved. *Elections don't change*
We need engaged citizens that will *who we are; elections*
love and serve their family and this *reveal who we are.*
country before and after going to the
polling place. Our civic duty is far more than voting; it is personally reflecting what we want in our nation so that together
we make a better nation. If you want a national turnaround, you

have to do more than vote and say someone else will fix it, you have to jump in yourself. If we want our government to do its job, we should also do our job of being the local role model fixing the local problems.

But, like a patient telling their doctor, "Something is wrong," we are a nation that feels something is "off" in America and it needs to be fixed right now. Elections always bring optimism for half the country and frustration for the other half. We want to stop the random violence, out-of-control immigration, crushing national debt, cultural decline, diminishing school achievement, and isolation. We want someone to get tougher. Yell louder. Fix all of it, in one big vote in Congress, right now. The most common questions I get as I travel around are, "How does this get better?" "When are we going to get mean like "they" are?" or my personal favorite, "Can you make it stop?"

We see the huge, huge national problems and feel that no one is really working to solve them fast enough; or even worse, some people are making the problems worse. That emotion makes us lash out at coworkers, friends, and family members in frustration. That, of course, makes the whole national situation even worse.

A few years ago, an Oklahoma Democrat constituent angrily walked up to me at the beautiful Oklahoma City airport and told me that she was a constituent and she felt I don't represent her progressive views, so she had no representation in Congress at all. After just a few seconds with this constituent, it was clear that we agree on almost nothing. *Two quick side notes:* Contrary to popular belief, yes, there are Democrats in Oklahoma (it's still legal), and I have learned that if a person starts the conversation with the words, "I am a constituent of yours," usually the conversation is about to go south pretty quickly. The good news is, we live in America. No one has to think alike, on the political right or left.

I asked her a couple of questions to hear her opinions. Then I asked, "Who in Congress shares your values and ideas?" She immediately named several of my very liberal counterparts in the Senate, whom I vote against every day (for good reason).

As an experiment, I asked whether she would be willing to keep talking until we found something where we agreed. We had ten minutes until our flight; surely, we could find something. We found we agreed on OKC Thunder basketball, several restaurants in town, multiple government oversight laws, the right of all citizens to one vote, the challenge of childhood poverty, and the major problem of our spiraling national debt (though we did not agree on the solution). We were also worried about the future of the country. The conversation moved from angry to engaging, which was so much better than angry belittling. When the volume is lower, sometimes people can hear each other out and solve the problem instead of yell about it.

We are a representative Republic. When you scan the 535 members of Congress and the rest of our government at all levels, you will find the attitudes and ethics of the people of the United States. Like it or not, Congress represents who we are, it's the big mirror to our nation. We have a diverse and combative government because our nation is diverse and combative, which is our free right, but it may not always be our best option. We need to fight for common-sense values and our future, but we should always fight to win.

I'M JUST A GUY

Depending on when we met, you would know me as a son, a husband, a dad, a student, a teacher, a pastor, the red-headed Falls Creek camp guy, or a member of Congress. My early story is a typical American story of the 1960s and '70s. My parents divorced when I was four. My mom moved my brother and me in with my grandparents until she could get on her feet again. We lived for years in a tiny one-bathroom rented house until my mom remarried eight years later, as I entered the sixth grade. (Middle school. What a great season of every boy's life!)

When I was eight years old, my life transformed with a simple revelation one Sunday: There is a God who made the world, and I did not yet know Him. When I accepted the love and forgiveness of Jesus, it changed me in more ways than I could ever describe on a page. That decision still affects my daily outlook and my future hope. I'm a firm believer that your faith should affect every road, relationship, or reaction, every day of your life. If your faith only affects your schedule on weekends, that's not a faith; that's a hobby. If you are more committed to your politics than your faith, then politics is your faith, and government is your hope.

My extraordinary mom had a deep personal faith in Jesus that gave her an adventurous and optimistic hope. Since she was a single mom and public school librarian, she "voluntold" me in the library helping her reshelve books all the time. To this day, I can't stand it when someone puts something in the wrong place. Everything has a right place, and it should be in that right place. Mom also pushed me to research, ask questions, and think about issues from someone else's point of view. As you can imagine, I heard the words "Look it up" more than once from my librarian mom.

As you can already tell, I was the nerdy kid growing up. I started organized debate in the fourth grade, band in the sixth grade, and Latin Club in high school. I was the kid in elementary school who knew how to correctly thread the film projector on the classroom AV cart—I assume at least half of the people reading this book have no idea what a film projector cart is, which is a good thing.

> *If your faith only affects your schedule on weekends, that's not a faith; that's a hobby.*

Years later, I finished graduate school with more than a degree; I also left with a beautiful bride. Cindy is a truly remarkable lady and leader. We had been the best of friends since we were sophomores in high school, but frankly, I never thought we would date. She was way out of my league. Cindy was too smart, gorgeous, and together to date a guy like me. Besides, she knew me from my nerd days (as if that has ever changed). When we finished high school, we went to different colleges for undergraduate work and master's programs, but lucky for me, we stayed in touch. We moved from lifelong friends to dating when Cindy was finishing her master's in speech language pathology, and I was working on my master's in Divinity (Theology).

I proposed in November, and we were married the following May. Together, we committed to serve God and each other for life. Two daughters and more than three decades later, we are still serving God, and each other, every day. When people ask us how long we have been married, our favorite way to answer is, "Not long enough!"

I served twenty-two years in ministry, mostly with teenagers. Thirteen of those years, I had the privilege of directing Falls Creek, the largest youth camp in America with around 51,000 teenagers during the eight weeks of the summer. For anyone who wants to see lives and families healed through spiritual transformation, Falls Creek is the greatest place on earth to serve.

By now, you are probably trying to figure out the political pedigree and political establishment figures who recruited us to run for the United States Senate; you couldn't find them if you tried. They don't exist. No one in my family is in politics, no one around us had served in politics, and no one approached us to run for Congress. In fact, no one expected it, including us. I'll explain more later, but for now, just know that resigning a position that I loved at the Falls Creek camp to step into the angry, chaotic world of D.C. politics was not what we anticipated in that season of our lives. The political world was not our "happy place." Much of Washington eats deception for breakfast, betrayal for lunch, and bitterness for dinner. That is not a table I wanted to put my feet under, but it's the place where I have the joy of serving today.

We are convinced that our lives, our families, and our nation will be better when average Americans love God, love people, and build community. Anyone can serve God and serve the remarkable and diverse people of the United States at the same time because the Constitution has no conflict with the Bible. I'm part of our Republic, just like you. We each hold a part of the history and the future of America. We have the freedom of faith, free speech, freedom of assembly, a free press, and free elections. Those freedoms allow us to vote and to choose who we will be as a nation every day.

WHERE ARE WE GOING?

Americans, on average, attend church less, volunteer less, and give less to non-profits than in previous years. A typical American now donates less than 2 percent of their income to nonprofits. We have more personal debt and less satisfaction than just a decade ago. A recent Gallup poll noted that less than 20 percent of Americans are satisfied with the way things are going in America. In another poll from the Trafalgar Group, 72.5 percent of voters believe America is in a state of cultural and economic decline. One election will not fix this; we need a turnaround.

We are a wealthy nation with thousands of options and opportunities, but 70 percent of Americans still believe we are on the wrong track. That 70 percent dissatisfaction is not about an election result, it's a result of our culture and our direction. Americans have more options for social media, sports, education, and energy drinks than anyone else in the world. We have over 310 million smartphones in America for around 340 million people. We have the most powerful military in the world, the largest economy in the world, the greatest number of innovations in the world, and yet the majority of Americans believe we are in "decline." We have consistently strived for more of everything, when our heart's desire is really for our nation to be good. We know in our collective gut that more is not better and louder is not better; *better* is better.

I recently had an interesting conversation with a former Australian ambassador to the United States. He told me, "America is a great country, but Americans are more critical of America than anyone else. The whole world looks up to

America, but Americans can't stop criticizing themselves." Then he said, "Americans need to lead again because the world is watching." It was a profound thought, but it sounded even more impressive with his thick Australian accent.

We know in our collective gut that more is not better and louder is not better; better is better.

No question, there is plenty of sordid content in our national history and current national story. However, we lead the world because our desire is always to be better, not just do better. It's deep in our DNA as Americans. We have pursued "a more perfect union" since the start. We are always working on "we." We are Americans. We are never content with where we are. There is always something else to be done.

That centuries-long drive has made us the envy of the world, but we also feel the effect of our growing apathy, debt, and division. We see fewer American flags flying, more government dependency, and a boiling anger just under the surface. We want wrong to be made right immediately, not in ten steps, but in one giant leap. We are better than our past and we are making progress, but it is painfully slow. Maybe it would help us regain a hopeful perspective to see how far we have already come. . . .

IN A CENTURY . . .

In the 1920s, tens of thousands of hooded Klansmen marched in cities across America, including Washington. At that time, the Ku Klux Klan stated that it had five million dues-paying members (in a nation of just over 100 million people). In 1924, the Democratic National Convention even voted down a resolution that opposed the Klan. America still has pockets of white supremacists spewing their division and hatred, but thankfully not like we did a century ago.

Just over 100 years ago, women could not vote in America. President Wilson initially ignored the women who protested for the right to vote in front of the White House, but he later had them arrested for "obstructing traffic" and put them in "the workhouse" for sixty days. They were considered "un-American" because they were protesting for suffrage during the bloody war in Europe. I guess President Wilson did not consider silencing peaceful protests as being "un-American."

In 1933, unemployment was at 25 percent. From 1929 to 1933, the gross domestic product (GDP = the total economic activity of the nation) fell by 29 percent. During that same time, a third of all banks closed. The economy collapsed. It was not a recession; it was a global depression, the "Great Depression."

Just over a century and a half ago, during the Civil War, more than 600,000 Americans died fighting each other in a hot shooting war from 1861 to 1865, followed by the assassination of the President and decades of Jim Crow racism and economic decline.

However, in the last century we also invented the computer, the digital watch, and the cell phone. We invented muscle cars, hybrids, and electric vehicles. We landed on the moon, created GPS, took pictures of distant galaxies, and even sent space tourists into orbit. Our research created breakthroughs in agriculture, healthcare, communication, artificial intelligence, photography, transportation, and energy. A century ago, many homes didn't have electricity, air conditioning, or indoor plumbing. None of them had broadband access, streaming services, or solar land-scape lights. A century ago, X was just a letter.

The D.C. swamp, and politicians in every state capitol, have more oversight, more transparency, and more account-ability than at any other time in American history. Every vote is live streamed, financial reports are required, and there are social media cameras everywhere. A century ago, corruption happened, but no one saw it. Now we see it and expose it immediately.

A century ago, the United States was struggling to find its place in the world. Today, billions of people across the globe wake up every day and want to be an American. Even all those Hollywood "stars" who claim they will move out of the country if a Republican gets elected President seldom actually do (unfortunately).

Without question, we are stronger, faster, and more comfortable than we were 100 years ago. We have made real progress, but there is so much more to do, and many Americans feel our heritage is slipping away. We cannot allow that to happen.

Previous generations did not always get it right, and neither will we. But we stand today on the sacrifice of Americans who loved and served our nation. Now, it's our turn to serve. We are the role models, Little League coaches, volunteers, military families, teachers, innovators, ministers, donors, builders, and leaders for our day.

Americans, in each generation, have done the work to fix the next problem. We don't just elect new leaders and expect them to do the work; we do the work together. Eisenhower didn't win the battle on D-Day; the American boys on the beaches of Normandy did. President Kennedy didn't build the Saturn V rocket; American scientists and engineers did. Leaders matter to the future of the nation, but the direction of the nation is set by "We the People."

Washington doesn't change the country; the country changes Washington.

Bad or good. Right or wrong. Angry or peaceful. Wise or foolish. Anchored or drifting. We decide our culture together. If we don't like who we have become, we are the only people who can change it.

The Trafalgar Group asked 1,000 Americans who is better suited to solve the problems we face as a nation: everyday Americans or elected officials? The response: 80.6 percent of voters believed everyday Americans are best equipped to reverse the state of cultural and economic decline in America. They are not wrong.

People tell me they feel powerless to fix our problems, but when they are asked who should fix it, Americans say, "We should." We know in our gut that we are not powerless and without options; we live in a Republic. We just must decide whether "Me the People" (that's you) will take the first step for "We the People" (that's us). For your family, your school, your neighborhood to get better, each of us needs to "get better." We each decide who "we" will be. We each set an example and a course for the nation based on our own actions and reactions.

> *Washington doesn't change the country; the country changes Washington.*

WHERE ARE YOUR EYES FOCUSED AND WHERE IS YOUR HOPE?

For centuries, when ancient Jewish worshipers traveled to Jerusalem for festivals or to offer sacrifice, as they approached the ancient holy city, they would sing the Psalms of Ascent, Psalms 120–134. Those Psalms were their traveling music, their public declaration of faith, and their preparation for worship. *As a side note,* each time I travel to Jerusalem, I read the Psalms of Ascent as I approach the city the first day. (To answer your next question, no I don't sing them; I just read them—that's mercy for the people around me.)

Psalm 121:1–5 stands out to me because of its declaration: "I lift up my eyes to the hills. From where does my help come? My help comes from the Lord, who made heaven and earth. He will not let your foot be moved; He who keeps you will not slumber. Behold, He who keeps Israel will neither slumber nor sleep. The Lord is your keeper . . . ." That's beautiful poetry and a powerful promise for Israel, but when you realize the context of Psalm 121, it's even more profound.

As the pilgrims approached Jerusalem thousands of years ago, there were two prominent buildings on top of the mountain, the Temple and the King's palace. As they looked at the beauty of both the palace and the temple, they declared, "My help comes from the Lord." They were literally saying that the palace is remarkable; it's the seat of the government God established. But their help was not in the government; their help came from the Lord.

Elected officials have very important, God-ordained tasks in our representative Republic, but so does each citizen. We should all acknowledge there is work to be done and government is not our savior. Our help comes from the Lord. So, let's pray and get to work on our individual and national turnaround.

2

WE THE PEOPLE

"We did it! We did it! Hooray!"

—DORA THE EXPLORER

Two letters make one word with a great deal of significance: *We.*

Though Thomas Jefferson had no part in the writing of the Constitution, the idea of "We the People" was built into the first lines of our Declaration of Independence when Jefferson wrote, "We hold these truths to be self-evident. . . ." In other words, this is what "we" believe. (Did I mention that Thomas Jefferson was a redhead? It's hard to tell on the $20 bill, but trust me, redheads recognize other redheads.)

Generations of Americans have loved, dreamed, and bloomed because "we" are all a part of our great nation. Our nation is a product of all of us and each of us. We certainly do not all agree, but we are still the people.

Each of us has influence for good or bad. It's likely that someone is watching you today as their example, which should either challenge you or terrify you, depending on your actions and example. I'm convinced Americans gripe about our culture not because we really think we are too far gone, but because we know we can be better. We believe our culture could improve, because deep, inside each of us knows we could improve. Each of us are the role model for the nation.

There had never been a nation built on "We the People" until our Constitution was ratified in 1789. Previous nations were built on one person or family who dominated everyone else or on loosely tied families or tribes who were disconnected from their neighbors. Monarchs like Alexander the Great and the Roman Caesars certainly spoke of the people, but the power remained centralized around them. That was true centuries ago, and it remains true today for billions of people around the world living in nations dominated by an elite group of "them." "We the People" was, and still is, a radical concept. Yet, that radical idea has become the most powerful economy and force for good the world has ever known.

The famous opening lines of our Constitution were a point of real debate and they went through significant changes as the Constitution was written in 1787. The concept of "We the People" and the following six purpose statements were not in the first draft of the writing and editing committees of the Constitution. (Yes, our Constitution was written by committees.) The Committee of Detail originally proposed more emphasis on the states by beginning the Constitution with "We the People of the States of . . . ," followed by a list of the thirteen states. The priority focus was the perspective of unique states, not individual citizens of a newly united nation.

When the Committee of Detail on August 6, 1787, passed its draft of the Preamble over to the Committee of Style for edits, the Committee of Style, led by Gouverneur Morris of Pennsylvania, changed the Preamble to what we now know, "We the People . . ." There is no record of why the Committee of Style edited the Preamble, but no doubt every kid in middle school civics class is glad they made it easier to memorize. Gouverneur Morris also added the six unique purpose statements to the Preamble, including ". . . to form a more perfect union, to establish justice, insure domestic tranquility, provide for the common defense, promote the general welfare and secure the blessings of liberty."

You may not know Gouverneur Morris's name, but he was a very influential leader at the Constitutional Convention and in the early days of our Republic. For a little background, his first name was Gouverneur, but he was not a governor. He grew up in a very wealthy British Loyalist family in Pennsylvania. In fact, while Gouverneur was fighting the British in the American militia, his mom allowed the British army to use their family farm as a base of operations. If you think it's tough when your family likes different football teams, imagine being on opposite sides of the American Revolution.

Gouverneur Morris was a lawyer, an assistant for the Treasury, and one of America's earliest ambassadors to France, during the French Revolution. He was the chairman of the Committee of Style for the Constitution. (Who wouldn't want to be known forever as the "Chairman of Style"?) He was exceptionally smart, with a reputation of being a little too blunt, and not always the best role model. But he trusted people to make the right choices. His focus on "we" as citizens determining the direction of the nation helped shape us into a country that would solve our problems, face our challenges, and cause us to rise or fall together.

Each word of our Constitution is important, but the emphasis on "We the People" has consumed our national psyche and set us on a common path for more than two centuries. We can make a more perfect union. We can establish justice. We can insure domestic tranquility. We can provide for a common defense. We can promote the general welfare of our fellow citizens. We can secure the blessings of liberty. We can do that. *We*.

THEM, I, OR WE?

Nations can be grouped into three broad categories: them, I, or we nations. Those three categories can define a huge nation or a small community. They could even define an individual family or workplace: them, I, or we.

Communities defined by "them" are dominated by a class of elites, gangs, or a single dictator and their preferred friends. They make the rules, run the show, and tell everyone else what to do. They are smarter than anyone else, more powerful than anyone else, and can tell the "others" what they should do and when they should do it. You can see this in dictatorial regimes like China and Iran and in workplaces and families where some get the benefits while others get ignored. Nations dominated by "them" may be orderly, but no one is free but the leaders.

Communities defined by "I" are self-serving places of greed and disorder where the focus is what I can get for myself, regardless of the pain suffered by my neighbors or fellow citizens. Life is about me and what I can get for me. I do whatever I want, because I deserve to get what I want, when I want it. In "I" cultures and politics, others are not important, only me and my wants.

When "we" defines the community, people live their daily lives to help their own families, establish leaders to get tasks done for the whole community, but also recognize the obvious fact that each person has a part to play in the lives of every other person. Nations are made from millions of individual "I's," but together they make a powerful "we" when serving your family, your neighbor, and your nation remains a priority. "We" can do amazing things when each "I" commits to "we."

Almost every time someone confronts me with caustic anger and says, "You have to do what I want because you work for me," I try to gently respond with, "I don't work for 'me'; I work for 'we.'" We don't all agree, but we must figure out how to work and live together. I do not live or think like my friends on the left and they don't live or think like my common-sense conservative approach to life.

Like it or not, we are stuck with each other, so we should sit down like adults and work out our differences. They are not going to run over me and my views and they are not willing to cave to mine. But they have as much right to their opinion as I have to mine. They have a story and a future, just like I do.

My wife and I enjoy handing out medals at the Oklahoma City Memorial Marathon. Standing at the finish line of a long race, you can feel the stories of the individual runners as they finish the final steps. Some have overcome injuries, surgery, cancer, or other traumatic life events, and you can see the determination as they complete the race.

If you are looking for a truly life-enriching marathon to run, put the Oklahoma City Memorial Marathon on your bucket list. Join us next April as we remember those who were lost, those who survived, and those who were changed forever after the Murrah Federal Building bombing, April 19, 1995. You will never forget the 168 seconds of silence at the start of the race near the bombing Memorial. You will be moved as you traverse through beautiful Oklahoma City, past the individual banners with the names of 168 people who were lost to domestic terrorism in 1995. Oklahomans remember the devastation caused by out-of-control anger toward government.

As the tens of thousands of runners from across the country move through the city in the cool April air, people stand on the sidewalks all over town and cheer. They don't ask the runners' position on any policy before they encourage them on the way; they just clap and shout to total strangers, "You are doing great! Keep going!" It's not that our national energy pol-

The experts and elected officials don't change the direction of the nation; "we" do.

icy doesn't matter; it does. It's not that a person's belief about the value of children in the womb is irrelevant; it's very relevant. It's not that the differing views on our national debt don't affect our children's future; they do. At that moment, we see people who need our encouragement as they do something difficult. We determine that we're going to serve our fellow Americans because they need it. That's America at our best, seeing people in need and serving them as we can.

We choose the direction of our nation through our votes and our daily lives. Voting certainly affects policy and the future progress of our nation. But each person, even those who don't vote, shapes the future of our country with their daily actions and attitudes. Every American can direct our nation toward a better, or worse, direction as they set the example for their family, neighborhood, or church. The experts and elected officials don't change the direction of the nation; "we" do.

I laugh (kindly, but I still laugh) when occasionally I hear people talk about the "experts" in government who can solve our challenging societal problems. Let me tell you, I have met many of the experts in the agencies of government; they are people just like everyone else. They may have a lofty degree and an area of expertise, but they have faults, challenges, biases, and preferences just like everyone else. Many of them work hard every day to serve their neighbors and fellow citizens. But they don't always get it right, and they are only a small part of "We the People."

In a Republic, people must be engaged and committed to being better, so the nation will be better. When individuals get better, our families get better. Then the community gets better. Then the government gets better. Remember, Washington doesn't change the country; the country changes Washington. We the People must set the example and lead.

We need more people to serve the nation in government, our communities, and our schools—in elected and career positions. Too many people spend their time criticizing everything and everyone in government, which discourages anyone sane from serving in government. Without question, there are some folks in government who need to be fired. However, if we want good government, we should encourage the good people already serving and challenge good neighbors to step up.

There's a basic principle of economics: If you tax something more, you get less of it. That principle also applies to life and service; if you discourage more, you get less of it. After the "defund the police" movement, fewer people applied for law enforcement jobs. In communities where teachers are publicly criticized day after day, schools have teacher shortages. When there is constant criticism of people serving in government, fewer good people want to serve in government. We all want to do something that is significant and appreciated, and there's no question, we need more great law enforcement, teachers, and people to serve our nation, at every level. So, we should find ways to encourage those who are doing a good job, while we call out those who are not. It's hard to step up if you know your only guarantee for the future is criticism.

THE SENATE IS THE PLACE
WHERE "WE" COLLIDE

We the People don't agree; that's obvious. It's our right, and frankly, it's our personality. I was a Pittsburgh Steelers fan growing up, just because all my friends were Dallas Cowboy fans. Yep, I was "that" kid.

America is big, diverse, and deeply divided on thousands of issues. But our differences need to be resolved, not just discussed. Thankfully, the Constitution created a place where "we" can resolve our divide, the United States Senate.

After the American Revolution, the United States operated under the Articles of Confederation. Our original attempt to organize the colonies into states had a weak central government with one legislative body. Any changes to the Articles of Confederation required a unanimous vote of all thirteen states, which, of course, meant there was never an amendment. Within a few years, it was clear this system of government was a failure. In 1787, the Constitutional Convention met in Philadelphia to determine how to fix our deadlocked system, which led to a new Constitution with two legislative bodies, a House and a Senate.

In 1788, eighty-five short essays, called the *Federalist Papers*, were published to convince states to ratify this new Constitution. Those papers are the best explanation we have for the original purposes of our government. In Federalist No. 62, James Madison made the argument for a "well-constituted"

Senate where Senators could study the law, challenge each other, and represent the various interests of their states. He argued that the Senate would be a place where "we" could discern together how to benefit every American, even with all our differences.

Of course, Madison wrote it more poetically when he outlined the design of the Senate in Federalist No. 62: "A good government implies two things: first, fidelity to the object of government, which is the happiness of the people; secondly, a knowledge of how that object can be best attained. Some governments are deficient in both these qualities; most governments are deficient in the first. I scruple not to assert, that in American governments too little attention has been paid to the last. The federal Constitution avoids this error; and what merits particular notice, it provides for the last in a mode which increases the security for the first."

While the United States Senate was designed as the place to settle our strong differences, it's also the epicenter of our national political frustration. From the first session of the Senate in 1789, a few Senators made very long speeches to express the opinion of their state and to prevent anyone else from speaking or voting. The early rules of the Senate did not allow a Senator to interrupt another Senator, so any one Senator could control the floor as long as they spoke.

In 1917, the Senate passed Rule 22, which created "cloture." Cloture provided a way to end the long speeches and force a vote, but two-thirds of the Senators had to vote to end the filibuster. In 1975, the Senate voted to reduce the number needed to end debate to three-fifths—sixty votes. The unique rules of the Senate are an American invention that ensures all sides are heard, no matter how long it takes to hear them. In other words, in America, "we" have a voice, even if "we" are in the minority. One side cannot just run over the other in the Senate. No other legislative body in the world has the same rules, it's uniquely American.

Not only are the rules different in our state legislatures, but the reality is also different. States are becoming less and less politically divided in their legislatures because they are less and less divided politically. When Americans get frustrated with their state government, we vote with our feet and a moving truck. In the 1930s, Oklahomans moved to California to find work during the Dust Bowl which was dubbed the "Grapes of Wrath" by John Steinbeck. Now, when Californians move to Oklahoma to escape high prices and over-regulation, I call it the "wrath of the grapes."

If we don't like the taxes, government, schools, crime, or attitude where we live, we move across the country to a place where people think like us. As people move to raise their family in a community that shares their values, more and more states have a "one-party" government system. Approximately four-fifths of our states now have the same political party in the governor's office and both bodies of their legislature. That's a significant change from just twenty-five years ago, when state leaders had frequent hard conversations in their divided state government.

It's absolutely the right and privilege of every free American to plant their family in the best place to match their values. But our mobility can increase the national political frustration. We get accustomed to local and state governments moving quickly on our preferred cultural and economic issues because of one-party rule. However, Washington is still very slow and divided because our nation is still very divided. Where we live, worship, or work, people mostly think alike, but it's crazy town a few states away and in Washington.

When it's time to decide a national issue, the Senate rules force leaders from all those one-party states to sit down in the same room and work out our differences in public. Even when the White House, House of Representatives, and Senate are of the same party, the Senate still requires bipartisan agreement because most bills need sixty votes to end debate.

The Senate is the one place in American government where the majority view cannot run over the minority opinion; both sides have a voice. That's incredibly, unbelievably, overwhelmingly frustrating when your party is in the majority, but it's also incredibly, unbelievably, overwhelmingly comforting when your party is in the minority. The Senate rules make it difficult to make law, but they ensure there is a place where all American opinions are heard.

The historic purpose of building American consensus in the Senate shouldn't be thrown away because it's in the way; it should cause us to remember why it's there. No political party has control of the levers of government for long in America; we should remember that before we change the rules to fit our short-term goals. Across the country and in the U.S. Capitol, "We the People" must persuade each other, not run over each other. Even when we win an election, we still have to keep persuading.

On his epically popular radio program, Rush Limbaugh publicly criticized conservatives in Congress and his friend, Speaker Newt Gingrich, for winning an election but losing the heart of the nation. In October 2010, Rush said, "The biggest mistake that was made after 1994 was that Newt and the boys believed that the country had gone conservative, and they stopped teaching. They removed all ideology from what they did. The reasons for doing things must always be explained. It's in the Constitution. It's in the best interests of the people. We care about people. We care about the country. We need to fix what's wrong. That's the biggest lesson of 1994."

Winning an election is an important first step to moving an idea in America, but there is more work to be done to move the country after the election. You can't just yell at or cancel the other point of view in the Senate and still pass legislation. The Senate rules force dialogue, which is why it's nicknamed "The world's greatest deliberative body." Unfortunately, recently the Senate seems to just complain about hard issues, instead of debating them, winning people over, and then resolving them.

Not all opinions are right, but all opinions have the right to be debated and decided in America. We protect the rights of the "other side," to voice their opinion even when they are clearly wrong because we want to make sure we protect our right to disagree when the "other side" is in control of government. I'm not afraid to kindly and boldly express my conservative point of view to win over people who disagree, because that is how we move ideas in America. At least that's how it was designed to work.

Sometimes, we complain but don't resolve the issue and it hurts every American. Gridlock has a cost. An obvious example of this is rising energy costs and diminishing energy supply in a nation with energy abundance.

Energy policy should start with a simple question: "We need more energy. How are we going to get it?" Instead, energy debates often start with the wrong question of, "What energy are we not going to use, regardless of what that does to prices or our economy?" If America needs more energy, which it does, then let's start talking about a plan of how to get more American energy. To be clear, my state of Oklahoma proudly has one of the most diverse energy portfolios in the country. We have low-cost, abundant, and reliable energy because we use gas, oil, wind, solar, hydro, geothermal, hydrogen, and coal. We even have nuclear power in our energy grid, though we don't actually produce the nuclear energy in Oklahoma. We actually believe in all of the above, and all of the below, energy production, since we see the obvious need for more energy.

Because of the fight over the energy sources not to use, most new energy projects get trapped in the mire of unwieldy federal regulations and legal challenges. Unlike the rest of the world, the United States foolishly takes years or decades to permit a new energy project, of any type. When permitting takes a decade, fewer people and companies invest in energy projects, because they have no idea if they will actually get a return on their investment. That, of course, leads to government giving more subsidies, more federal debt, and higher energy prices. Having less energy hurts Americans through higher prices now and a weaker economic future. Ten years ago, many companies advertised they only used renewable energy, but now they just want any reliable energy because the supply of energy is too low for our growing economy.

We have the ability to fix our energy permitting log-jam, but we can't seem to have a rational, fact-based conversation about our national energy requirements that starts with, "How do we get more energy?" Some people will not even consider all sources of energy because the hard-core left demands all energy must be from federally subsidized carbon-free energy. They ignore the facts that wind power requires massive amounts of oil to lubricate the turbines, electric vehicles use carbon for their batteries, and solar uses carbon-based mineral production to create the panels. This is not an insignificant debate since billions of people around the globe depend on American energy innovation and energy production.

Some activists have little to no appreciation for the rising cost of energy and the effect of energy inflation on working families. When pipelines cannot be built, new drilling leases cannot be purchased, and oppressive energy permitting drives up the price of production, and inflation increases as every product people buy costs more. The sun and wind may be free in nature, but wind and solar power cost billions of dollars in taxpayer subsidies, and they currently require Chinese-controlled minerals and manufacturing. Hydrogen is a reasonable fuel for some industrial use, but it requires massive new systems to produce it and the construction of a million miles of new pipeline to move it. Hydrogen production is also currently exceptionally inefficient since it uses almost as much energy in its manufacturing as it produces. We can and should use hydrogen in places where it makes sense, but it's not the answer to all our future energy needs.

I have no problem with any form of energy if it's reliable, affordable, and domestic. Unfortunately, at this moment, most renewable energy isn't any of those three, so we should be cautious before we put all our eggs in the Chinese renewable energy basket. Wind and solar are valuable supplements to our massive energy needs each day, but they cannot provide the base power we need all day, everyday. Anywhere you install wind and solar, you must also have natural gas, nuclear, coal, or other base power that's reliable when the wind stops and the sun sets.

No one disagrees that we should produce our energy in the cleanest method feasible, but we also should agree that we need more energy, not less, for our growing population and technology. We shouldn't raise prices for people on low and fixed incomes, dramatically increase our national debt, or make our country dependent on China for our daily energy needs. No one will ever convince me that buying critical minerals, batteries, oil, gas, or refined products from China, Venezuela, or the Middle East is environmentally cleaner, keeps us out of foreign conflicts, or increases American jobs. Americans don't want to be dependent each day on the benevolence of a distant communist regime so they can drive to work.

There are Senators who adamantly oppose my common-sense view of energy, but they fly to Washington on a jet that uses fossil fuels, drive in a car that uses fossil fuels (even if their car is electric, the anodes in the battery are made of carbon), and turn on the fossil fuel-powered lights in their Capitol office. They have carpet under their feet, paint on their walls, Wi-Fi on their devices, and climate control in their office because of fossil fuels. They speak on the floor of the Senate about the evils of carbon-based fuels, even when they have seen the data that proves there is no way to completely replace fossil fuels in the foreseeable future. But as we argue, prices go up, and the future supply gets more and more limited. Energy policy has to be rational, compassionate, and resolved now.

We are stewards of the planet we live on, but we are also families who live on a budget and want to turn down the AC in the summer and the heater up in the winter. The price of gas is almost three times higher in California than Oklahoma because of irrational regulations. Northeastern politicians who use home heating oil in their basement during the winter, want to impose electric vehicle mandates on rural Oklahoma farmers and ranchers. Activists regularly shut down construction of interstate pipelines and electrical power lines, which raises prices and diminishes reliability for everyone.

Unless you are naked, living in a tree, eating only nuts, you use fossil fuels.

As a friend of mine says, "Unless you are naked, living in a tree, eating only nuts, you use fossil fuels." Our energy policy should respect our environment while lowering prices, creating more source diversity, more domestic production, more national security, and more reliability. We can do all of that, if we will have a respectful, rational, data-driven discussion about how we develop more energy for our future. It's time for us to lay out the facts in a respectful dialogue and get America the energy we need to lead the world. We can do this.

HONOR

One very hot afternoon, in the crowded Ronald Reagan Washington National Airport, I was talking to someone from Oklahoma in the terminal as we both waited to board another flight home. If you have ever flown into or out of Ronald Reagan Washington National Airport, you know the terminal is a diverse mix of school-age tourists, corporate CEOs, elected officials, lobbyists, activists, federal employees, families coming to bury a loved one at Arlington Cemetery, farmers and ranchers coming to explain the farm bill to congressional staff, and thousands of other people from hundreds of other backgrounds. It's truly a slice of America crammed into one little space.

On this particular day, the flight was late, again, but as we waited in the crowded terminal, a man with a huge hand bell began to ring it and yell, "Hear ye, Hear ye, Hear ye!"—which is serious old-school Washington. He asked everyone in the terminal to please welcome the men and women arriving who were on an Honor Flight to visit the war memorials on the National Mall. A plane full of men and women who were veterans of World War II, the Korean War, and the Vietnam War began walking up the jet bridge into the airport terminal. Without hesitation, everyone stopped their conversations and began to cheer as the veterans walked into the crowd. The sound of the applause was deafening and beautiful. Men and women in their seventies, eighties and nineties wept as they walked through the crowded terminal and looked into the faces of total strangers cheering their sacrifice.

At that moment, everyone was an American, and we were grateful. We disagreed on some things, but we all agreed we should cheer for honorable people who had put their lives on the line so we could live free.

Lately, we seem to lead with our differences, instead of our common connection. Our differences are real and we shouldn't just ignore them. (I can't just pretend any and every idea or choice is a good idea or choice.) But we also shouldn't live in the metaphorical hot, crowded apartment building located at 666 Perturbed Street, where we just argue but never resolve. We can and should fight for what we believe, with the goal of solving the challenges of our nation, not just yelling about the problems.

We can fix what is broken and make a more perfect union. We can do this—we are Americans.

Let's get practical and start thinking through how we can make a better "we."

3

SEE A PROBLEM,
BE THE LEADER

---

*"A great leader's courage to fulfill his vision
comes from passion, not position."*

—JOHN C. MAXWELL

The Chuck Wagon Diner was the place to be for breakfast. It was a small place, but plenty big enough for Sperry, Oklahoma, population just over a thousand really nice people. Sperry is close enough to Tulsa, Oklahoma, to drive in and get anything you need, but far enough away to not see any city lights at night. In the back of the restaurant, there was a gathering of good folks with white hair solving the world's problems over pancakes and eggs at the "Round Table" (which was actually a big oval). There were plenty of great conversations all around the Chuck Wagon Diner, but if you wanted to sit at the Round Table, you should have had thick skin and a great sense of humor. When members of the Round Table breakfast group passed away, their names were written on the "Round Table Heroes" list on the wall next to the table. That allowed the guys to keep being at breakfast, without actually being at breakfast.

One morning, I was a guest at the Round Table, and one of the guys told me the smartphone was the worst thing ever invented. When I asked why, he told me that they used to sit around the table arguing about something for weeks, but when the smartphone came along, now someone just looks up the answer, and the argument is over. As he said, "The smartphone killed all our good fights over breakfast."

Funny thing about the members of the Round Table. They laughed and they talked about everything and everyone in Sperry, but they also quietly worked together to figure out how to solve some of the problems in town. They secretly donated money to people, fixed broken things for the city, and found ways to be the community heroes before they ended up on the wall as "Heroes." They were just normal good folks who figured out how to lead by serving.

I have no idea how many times I've sat with a group of neighbors at a restaurant as we've talked about the weather, rising prices, government failures, and our deplorable culture. It is a typical American conversation over breakfast until someone asks, "What should we do about it?" Then people look around at each other and ask for their check so they can leave. When it's time for a leader, some people look for the door.

GRIPING IS NOT FIXING.
FIXING IS FIXING.

Anyone can complain; leaders decide to do something about it. When a family fights all the time, someone needs to sit down with everyone and make peace. When there are problems at the school, someone should step up and serve. When a church is busy, but not productive, someone needs to help set a new direction. When people at the office, shop, or store are whining about what should be done, but no one is willing to do it, clearly leadership is needed. When we need good people to run for election, good people need to take the risk to run. When good people need help running for election, someone needs to volunteer alongside them. But, to be clear, being elected doesn't make you a leader; being a leader makes you a leader.

Some people refuse to step out and lead because it takes time and risk. Leaders can get it wrong. The community sometimes demands perfection from leaders, though not from themselves. Criticizing leaders has become a sport in America. When I posted about our family dog dying in 2024, there were several people who lashed out at me

If you live to please everyone all the time, you will not lead anywhere or anytime.

in the comments. Talk about kicking someone when they are down. There are some gripey folks out there in social media land who need to get a life and a little compassion.

I receive tens of thousands of emails and phone calls every year, both encouraging and critical. One day, a man emailed my office to let me know he watches my interviews on TV, and he wanted to know why I switched to a half-Windsor knot for my tie and had lately stopped using a full-Windsor knot. He told me that a half-Windsor knot was a lazy way to tie a tie. Two thoughts came to mind that day: (1) Some ties work better with a half-Windsor knot, based on the weight of the fabric, and (2) this guy needs a different hobby. Literally, no matter what you do in leadership, you will be criticized. If you live to please everyone all the time, you will not lead anywhere or anytime.

Truthfully, "leadership" can be an intimidating word. Many people are not willing to see themselves as a leader. Someone else always has more experience, money, power, and influence. We think, "I'm just plain old me." Leadership feels like something big that you must live up to, gain with prestige, or be born into.

Would you be willing to consider a simple new definition of leadership? Leadership is seeing a problem and then finding some people to help you do something to solve it. Leaders build teams to solve problems; it's not that complicated. If you know someone who would help you work on a problem you both see, then you are a leader. You may not have a leadership title, but you are a leader. If you need a leadership title, declare yourself emperor of the task, and start getting it done. Who wouldn't follow the neighborhood emperor?

It's almost certain that if you are reading a book like this, you already see some things around you that need to change. It's also likely that you could text a few people right now and ask them to help you work on it. That means you are a leader or a potential one, if only you would start sending those texts. Sometimes the only difference between a leader and a potential leader is the decision to stop complaining and start working. Try it. Pull out your phone right now and ask someone to join you in helping someone else. Pick any problem to work on, small or large, and see what happens next.

> *Leadership is seeing a problem and then finding some people to help you do something to solve it.*

IF IT BUGS YOU, THEN IT IS YOUR PROBLEM

On the street outside our neighborhood, there is a low spot that collects trash blowing down the street. It's along the edge of our neighborhood, so it's not the city's problem, but it's outside the neighborhood, so it's not the neighborhood's problem either. However, it's still trash that needs to be cleaned up. I noticed it for months as it got worse and worse. One day when I was driving the girls to school, I made a dad declaration: "We are going to clean up that trash." The two girls in the back seat suddenly gave their clear vocal response to the thought of collecting trash along the side of the road that leads toward their school. If you're a parent, you know well the response was not joy or excitement coming from the back seat.

Picking up trash near your house isn't all that exciting or world-changing. It's just a dirty job that needs to be done when you are a good neighbor. It took us thirty minutes, but it sent a message to my daughters that serving others is a part of leading and making our nation and community better. It was also a simple way to serve everyone and lead by example.

Maybe picking up trash for me was a type of penance. When I was a kid, I could walk past the dog poop at home twenty times and not mention it, because I knew if I were to mention it, I would have to clean it up. So, my brother and I would walk past the mess and never "see" it. No way, not my problem. Except it was my problem; I just ignored it.

Leaders see a problem and take the responsibility to work to fix it, no matter the size of the problem. You don't wait for the big problem; you work on whatever the problem is nearby. Some people want a big following online so people will know their name. But leading is not about popularity or fame; it's about service and solutions. When you lead, you recruit others to help others. That's the gift of leadership;

They saw a problem, decided to do something about it, asked a few people to help, and got it done. That's leadership.

you not only help someone right now, but also help other people develop a heart to lead for the future.

If you ask most of the people you see as leaders today how they started, you will probably hear their story of being faithful in a few small things that grew over time to something large. Their friends or their family caught the vision and decided to help, and the small thing began to grow large. They started volunteering after school with a friend. They paid something forward in a small way that caught on in a big way. They started posting good ideas and grew their platform consistently and constantly. They saw a problem, decided to do something about it, asked a few people to help, and got it done. That's leadership.

POCKET FULL OF HOPE

In 1999, Lester Shaw sat in an education conference listening to a lecture about pockets of poverty and pockets of crime in our communities. No question—every city and community in America has pockets of struggle that need focus and compassion. That day, he wondered why no one seemed to talk about pockets of hope in our community. Instead of wondering, he decided to call a few friends and see if they could be the people to bring hope. He already was a busy educator, but he made time after school to start Pocket Full of Hope in the Historic Greenwood District of North Tulsa. It was a simple idea, really. Engage a few youth with music, dance, photography, and videography to help them stay in school, find purpose, create opportunities, and develop leadership. In short, provide a pocket full of hope. It was only a few kids, but it could make a difference for them, and their future.

More than two decades later, Pocket Full of Hope has mentored over 5,000 youth and has a 100 percent high school graduation rate. Let that soak in for a moment—a 100 percent graduation rate. Pocket Players, those who aged out of the program, come back and mentor the younger students to demonstrate what hope looks like with skin on. Pocket Players are in leadership roles across the nation, maybe in a company you know or work with right now.

For years, Pocket Full of Hope met in an older house that had lots of love but was a little run-down. Over time, as the Pocket Full of Hope grew, the old house became way too small for the task. Lester and his wife, Brenda (who is also an educator), prayed and worked to create a better place for the youth of North Tulsa. Their attention kept turning toward an abandoned warehouse that in its glory days was the Big 10 Ballroom, where black artists like Ray Charles, Count Basie, Ella Fitzgerald, Otis Redding, Ike and Tina Turner, James Brown, and many others performed during the Civil Rights era. But that was years ago. Now, the old Big 10 building needed its own pocket full of hope. After more than a decade of sweat, prayer, and tears, the Shaws reopened the Historic Big 10 Ballroom to provide a better space for mentoring students. Music echoes in the rafters again at the Historic Big 10.

If you meet Lester Shaw, and I hope you get the privilege, you will find he is a remarkable leader. He stepped up to do what everyone knew should be done but did not want to do the work required. He is different because he was willing to pray and then actually do it. He did not set out to rebuild the Big 10 Ballroom or mentor thousands of students; he just started mentoring a few students and remained faithful to his calling each day. No money, no long-term strategy, no fancy office; just a calling, tenacity, and hope. He did not whine; he worked. He led not because it was easy, but because it was right. He is not a perfect man; he is just a man who determined something should be done, so he did it.

Leadership is not complicated; it's getting off the couch and doing something with someone for somebody. Most of the time, a shortage of resources isn't the problem; a shortage of leaders is. Everyone sees the problem, but very few people will do something about it.

We usually look around for people with titles to fix problems. However, the people with the titles may have already decided they are not going to solve that problem, or they may be so overwhelmed with their other responsibilities that they just can't add another one. So the problem remains. Titles don't fix problems; leaders fix problems.

Most places desperately need a role model and problem solver, but few people will take the risk to lead. They don't feel worthy, empowered, or equipped; so they watch the problem, talk about the problem, but don't try to solve the problem. Sitting back and complaining will only make you bitter or apathetic. God laid that issue on your heart for a reason; go solve it.

He did not whine; he worked.

If you are a person who believes leadership is for someone else, you missed the point. You have a calling and a task that's just for you. Our nation needs you to take a risk and serve others in practical ways. We need you in the battle with us. See a problem; decide to do something about it; ask a few people to help you get it done. Be the leader.

We were not meant to ignore the challenges around us and just hope they get better; we were meant to take them on. We fight to make life better. Every time we see a problem and work to solve it, our heart pounds with meaning, fulfillment, and purpose. However, every time we see a problem and look away, our heart for the hurting hardens a little more, our possessions take on less meaning, and our life feels less purposeful. We are at our best when we each boldly and respectfully live our values, because that not only reinforces the truth in

> *Every time we see a problem and work to solve it, our heart pounds with meaning, fulfillment, and purpose.*

our own life, it encourages others to live the truth out loud in their life.

DRIFTING

In 1985, a ten-year-old boy on vacation with his family wrote a message, put it in an empty Pepsi bottle, threw it into the Atlantic Ocean, and watched it drift away from the Florida coast. Almost four decades later, after a hurricane, it washed ashore just twelve miles from where he had thrown it into the ocean. In thirty-seven years, it traveled twelve miles. Before you write me about the complexities of ocean currents, let me finish my thought.

Sailors can circumnavigate the globe in a sailboat in less than half a year (the record is forty-one days). But sailors have purposeful direction—they harness the power of the wind and currents to go somewhere, intentionally. They know where they are going, and they stay focused to get there.

A Pepsi bottle floating in the ocean is not headed anywhere, and it will not make a difference, even if it has a great message, because it's just drifting. It's not trying to accomplish anything other than staying afloat. Drifting is easy. We end up where and when we end up.

That seems to define America today. The greatest nation in the world, with a message of freedom, values, and opportunity, is drifting instead of intentionally sailing. The mixed messages to our youth, a rapidly growing national debt, and a diminished commitment to our foundational values have disconnected us from our solid mooring. No one drifts toward better; we drift toward decline.

In the spring of 2019, record rainfall throughout northern Oklahoma and southern Kansas overfilled all the lakes in northern Oklahoma and pushed the Arkansas River past its limits in unprecedented ways. The river at Three Forks, less than a half mile upstream of the Port of Muskogee, crested approximately twenty-four feet above normal. The critical McClellan-Kerr Arkansas River Navigation System inland waterway, nicknamed MKARNS, and the multiple ports that it serves in Oklahoma were inundated. The water in the river was so far out of bank that even the port offices in Muskogee were under water.

At the height of the flood, the rail dock sank at the Port of Muskogee, and two barges, loaded with fertilizer, started drifting downstream in the floodwaters toward the Webbers Falls Lock and Dam. Operators worked frantically to get control of the barges in the fast-moving water after they broke loose from the mooring dolphins (the tie-off anchors, not the cute ocean mammals). The operators even tried to tie off the drifting barges to a huge oak tree on the bank. But the force of the water pulled the giant oak out of the ground and dragged the entire tree, roots and all, downstream with the barges.

The floodwater flowed past the river gauge at a rate of 506,999 cubic feet per second. To give you some reference for the math junkies, 1 cubic foot per second = 7.4805 gallons flowing by a particular point in 1 second, which means the river water was flowing at 3,792,606 gallons per second. The awe-inspiring Horseshoe Falls at Niagara Falls flows at 681,750 gallons per second, which meant the water flowing down the Arkansas River that day, just south of Tulsa, Oklahoma, flowed more than five times faster than Horseshoe Falls. Way too fast for a tugboat to control a barge. It was a bad day to drift.

On May 23, 2019, both barges, full of fertilizer, slammed into a lock and dam and sank to the base of the dam within one minute. It was a total loss for both barges and all their cargo. It also shut down the entire MKARNS inland waterway for six months while crews worked to clear the wreckage and get the locks operable. Pool 16 had to be "de-watered" to make the repairs, which put the Port of Muskogee out of business for months.

Did I mention that it was a bad day to drift?

The inland waterway and its mooring dolphins were installed in the late 1960s because local, state and federal leaders knew the Midwest would need flood control and port access. If they had not done the critical work decades before, the flood would have been even worse that day. However, it was clearly time for a new vision.

All the operators, leadership, and champions for the river in Oklahoma put together a Waterways Action Plan, and they started practicing with emergency responders to prepare for the next flood. They were determined that Oklahoma would be ready next time. Leaders on the ground went to work with local, state, and federal partners to build new beacons, mooring dolphins, and flood protection. They didn't throw up their hands and say, "It's a flood; nothing can be done," or "Someone in Washington needs to come fix everything." Oklahomans got busy stopping future drifting and destruction on the river. The disaster brought them together with greater focus for the future.

MORAL COURAGE

Every state has two statues of leaders their state has chosen to honor in the United States Capitol. On May 16, 2024, North Carolina removed one of its statues of a former governor, who had been a segregationist scoundrel, and replaced it with a seven-foot-high bronze statue of Billy Graham pointing to an open Bible. The dedication ceremony in the Capitol was a fitting tribute to a man who lived a life of integrity, committed to the truth of a very simple verse, "For God so loved the world that He gave His one and only Son, that whoever believes in Him shall not perish but have eternal life." John 3:16.

Billy Graham was, without question, one of the most influential voices in the twentieth century. No one would have believed what he would become as he grew up during the Depression on a family dairy farm, just outside of Charlotte, North Carolina. His "breakout" crusades in the late 1940s and 1950s were held in Los Angeles, New York, and London, not exactly the most likely locations for a dairy farmer kid from rural North Carolina.

There were a myriad of stories, godly advice, and wise words from Billy Graham that were shared during the dedication ceremony of his larger-than-life statue. He was a counselor to thirteen Presidents, a preacher to more than 200 million people in person, and a role model for a generation. Some may not realize that he was also a leadership coach to millions. In an article in *Reader's Digest*, July 1964, he said, "Courage is contagious. When a brave man takes a stand, the spines of others are often stiffened." He also reminded the readers, "Moral courage has rewards that timidity can never imagine."

Not a bad leadership reminder for today. If you ever have the opportunity to walk into the United States Capitol, I hope you take the time to find the Billy Graham statue and read the scripture on the pedestal where he stands. It would be a good way to reflect on what you could do to also set a future example of servant leadership.

4

ANCIENT LEADERSHIP LESSONS

---

*"Stand at the crossroads and look;
ask for the ancient paths,
ask where the good way is,
and walk in it, and you will find
rest for your souls."*

—JEREMIAH 6:16

Several years ago, my younger daughter, who was in high school at the time, bought her first car, which she promptly named "Chandler." It was a used, in fact very used, Nissan Versa. It had high mileage, a small dent on the hatch, the apron under the front of the car hung down a bit, and the vinyl covering the passenger armrest had serious issues, but the car was hers, all hers. The car ran great, except for one annoying mechanical quirk: the AC. It blew cold air, but if you turned the air conditioning fan to "high," it would repetitively click, really loudly. Thankfully, there was an easy "fix": Keep the AC on low. Unfortunately, in Oklahoma summers, low AC is not as helpful. She just lived with it, for years.

One day, the world changed. The AC started clicking so loudly that it moved from a bother to intolerable. The low air was now cold and loud. Chandler needed some undivided attention. As you could imagine, it also became the embarrassing feature of her first car. It was time for Dad to stop doing nothing and start doing something.

I did what every shade-tree mechanic dad does. I started searching YouTube to see if anyone else had this problem and if they knew how to fix it. To my surprise, I couldn't find anyone else online who had experienced this problem. Surely, we were not the first to have this odd clicking. At least I found a video to help me find the blower motor. Since the noise increased when we turned up the fan speed, I assumed the problem had to be there.

Try to picture my contortions as I lay on my back in the fully reclined front passenger seat of my daughter's car, my head to the floorboard, face to the dashboard, feet sticking over the seat, trying to reach my right arm into the tiny area under her dash. Then imagine my shock when I removed the fan blower and discovered an entire pecan inside it, still in the shell. How in the world did a whole pecan get into her fan blower?! Maybe it was a very effective squirrel hiding nuts. Of course, if it was a squirrel, which it probably wasn't, I'm sure when he hid that pecan, his skinny little arm fit more easily under the dash of her car than mine.

What took me less than two hours to fix in the driveway had been a problem my daughter had endured for years. The problem finally became so loud, we could not ignore it any longer. Enough was enough; action was required. Something had to be done.

We seldom fix family, national, or cultural problems when they are small and easy; we usually procrastinate until they are loud. For years, our national problem with federal debt, illegal immigration, energy production, overregulation, and much more goes on and on. People complain, often correctly, that Congress ignores problems until they are too loud to ignore. But before we say this is only a Congressional problem, think how often some people ignore for years bad relationships at work, a distant marriage, or a stagnant personal faith. The problems that persist are the problems we are willing to ignore.

When we finally acknowledge a problem, we have three choices: Are you going to do everything, do at least something, or do nothing about the problem? Everything is often really tough, something doesn't seem like enough, so unfortunately nothing is typically the easy default. When the paint color is out of date in the kitchen, it's easy to do nothing for years, because if you change the paint, you may need to also change the counter-top or the cabinets. If you change the cabinets, you may need to change the oven, but if you change the oven, it will not match the other appliances. Suddenly, it's so much easier to just do nothing because you can't do everything. In our health, our family, our community, or our nation, the same options are repeated over and over—do everything, do something, or do nothing. Doing nothing is always easy, but it's seldom the right answer.

> *When we finally acknowledge a problem, we have three choices: Are you going to do everything, do at least something, or do nothing about the problem?*

Serving in Congress for over a decade, I have seen the everything, something, or nothing decision process play out innumerable times. It's a painful cycle when you want problems solved. Doing everything to solve a major problem is complex, so Congress rarely does the intense cooperative work. When the problem is severe, doing only something doesn't seem like enough, so Congress defaults back to nothing (which is certainly worse). Of course, doing nothing is easy, which is a skill Congress has honed for years.

I guess I should not say members of Congress do nothing; they do press conferences, write strong bills they know will not pass, post on social media, and give impassioned speeches. So, at least there is an acknowledgment of the problem. But press conferences and social media posts don't solve the problem; they only point out the problem. Admitting there is a problem may be the first step in a twelve-step program to recovery, but it doesn't automatically lead to a resolution in Congress. It takes only one person to give a press conference, but in the United

States Senate, it takes sixty people to start making a law. That requires doing more than talking; it requires sitting down with people you disagree with and working to solve the problem.

AN ANCIENT EXAMPLE OF
SOMEONE WHO DID SOMETHING

I have a confession. I am obsessed with the biblical story of Nehemiah. It's a larger-than-life story and a great lesson on leadership, sacrifice, and calling. It's the story of a guy who heard about a problem, prayed about it, and then decided something had to be done to solve it. The ancient Nehemiah leadership principles are as current as the latest social media post, with one exception: Unlike a social media post, what Nehemiah did and said was true and important.

A quick history lesson is needed to get the context of this ancient story from more than two and a half millennia ago. For more than 500 years, Jews had lived in the land of Israel, but in 722 BC, the Assyrians conquered the ten tribes in the northern section of Israel called Samaria. A century and a half later, in 586 BC, the remaining two southern tribes were destroyed by the Babylonians. When the southern tribes were conquered, the skilled laborers, educated, and leadership were all taken into captivity and put into re-education camps to be trained in the culture of the Babylonians as they prepared for their new life in slavery. The poorest of the poor Jews were left to scrape by in Jerusalem after the city was devastated. They had no protection from the surrounding threats. As time passed, the Babylonians were overtaken by the Medes and Persians, who inherited all the

Babylonian slaves, including the Jews. Did I mention, the region around Israel was a tough neighborhood even 2,000 years ago?

As the Book of Nehemiah begins, it's around a century after the fall of Jerusalem. None of the Jews in captivity grew up in Israel; they were all born in slavery. They had no hope and no future. In the opening lines of the story, Hanani, Nehemiah's brother, is returning from Jerusalem. We don't know why he went there, but his brother Nehemiah is intrigued with the situation in the land of their ancestors, Jerusalem.

Most likely, Nehemiah knew little about the people and place where his ancestors lived, but he still had a spiritual and emotional connection to Jerusalem. It was important to him, even if the city was in shambles.

When Nehemiah asked his brother a simple question, "What's it like in Jerusalem?" Hanani answered that the people are "living in disgrace, the walls are down, and the gates have been burned." A century before, Jerusalem had been a bustling walled city with a long Jewish heritage, but now there was little to no economy and the wall was destroyed. In other words, the people there were living in abject poverty, and they were totally defenseless. Basically, Hanani said, "It stinks to be them." Then he walked away.

But while Hanani ignored the problem and walked away, Nehemiah could not shake it. He knew something needed to be done, but he wasn't a government leader or an engineer. He was an expendable slave to a king who could care less about an old run-down Jewish city he had inherited. Nehemiah chose to go to his knees and pray about it for days, and he asked God what he should do. God gave Nehemiah a plan and the favor of the king to get it done. Remarkably, months later, when Nehemiah laid out his proposal to the king, he was allowed to temporarily leave his position to go help rebuild Jerusalem. Nehemiah saw the problem, prayed about the problem, and then he got to work doing something. Not a bad formula.

Within months, the person who knew little about Jerusalem was headed to help the people in the city get back on their feet. When Nehemiah arrived, he organized each family to start rebuilding the defensive walls around Jerusalem. He knew they could not rebuild their economy and bring stability if they could not stop the constant threats and raids on their families and property. In ancient times, and modern, you cannot have a growing economy without security. *Just as a side note,* walls are still not a terrible idea. We still put fences around backyards, around government buildings, and on our national border to deter anyone from wandering onto our property.

There are many great leadership principles in the opening of the story, but the key point for this chapter is still coming. When Nehemiah arrived in devastated Jerusalem, he surveyed the situation, and then he organized a plan for the people to identify the pieces of the ancient broken wall that were near their house and start rebuilding. Many families had lived for a century literally next to the broken, but fixable, ruins of the wall, but they never repaired it. There were also Jews who lived nearby who were willing to volunteer to rebuild the ancient city, but they never organized for the work until Nehemiah called them to the task. When they all worked together, they re-established their defenses in less than two months. For years, they had everything they needed to restore the wall, except someone who would stop complaining about the broken wall and start leading them to fix it.

Before I get overly critical of the people of Jerusalem procrastinating more than 2,500 years ago, I need to confess my own propensity to put things off that are broken. It is easier to walk past a burned-out light, a creaking door, a wall in need of paint, or a million other things, when they become familiar. Real estate agents always want a fresh set of eyes to look over your house before you list it. There are usually problems you don't see anymore because you have grown accustomed to them. Broken is normal when you live with a problem for too long. That's a risk for all of us. We should not allow ourselves to accept broken as normal. Especially when it is our nation. Broken marriages, neighborhoods, schools, families, workplaces and governments should awaken us to the need for our action and a national turnaround. In America, broken should be fixed, not ignored.

> *Broken is normal when you live with a problem for too long.*

The first principle of leading is seeing the problem; the next is getting others to help you solve it. Nehemiah checked both of those boxes. Nehemiah didn't see the problem as too big. He didn't see himself as too unqualified. He seemed to understand that God had put that specific problem on his heart for a reason, so he prayed and got to work.

Nehemiah had a simple plan; each person should start fixing the section of the broken wall next to their own house. How revolutionary. Work on the problems around you and encourage others to work on the challenges next to them and see what happens. You can't do everything, but you should at least do something, instead of doing nothing. Genius!

The challenges of our nation may not be physically next door to your house (or they may be), but some will certainly be in your circle of influence and travel. What problem exists around you that could really use a leader to fix? Are you willing to do something to help solve the problem, even though it may not be everything?

In my position as a Senator, I have the privilege of meeting so many great people in my home state of Oklahoma and around the country. People from every political background catch me at a restaurant with my family, at church, or in the grocery store and want to talk about the challenges in our nation, sometimes at the most awkward moments.

One day I left Home Depot with a new toilet that I was replacing in my bathroom—I had cracked the previous one when I had screwed it down too tight to the floor, a total rookie mistake that had cost me 150 bucks. As I pushed my cart out of the store with a shiny white toilet in it, like a port-a-john for an exhibitionist, a total stranger stopped me in the parking lot and wanted to talk national politics and her ideas. Not the best moment to chat. I don't often speak for all my colleagues, but I can confidently say, if you ever run into your Senator while they are pushing a shopping cart with a commode, they don't want to talk politics right then.

When most folks ask what they can do to help the country, I usually tell them to care for their family, volunteer at their church, give time to a local nonprofit, or run for school board. (For the record, they usually then ask me if there is anything else, besides those things, they can do.) If you want to do something big, fix the problems right next to your house first.

I am clearly not opposed to anyone going on mission trips around the world or working on challenges a thousand miles away. But someone who will only serve far away while ignoring next door has missed a basic truth: If each of us serves the people nearby, we will make a huge difference nationally.

The heroes in my community are volunteers at local non-profits that mentor the homeless, walk with moms and dads at a pregnancy resource center, and minister to families experiencing deep poverty and hopelessness. I really enjoy meeting people who are providing food to the hungry because they have a special glow about them. They are making a difference, and they know it.

Complaining about schools is in vogue right now. However, griping is not the gift schools need; they need volunteers, donated supplies, and encouragement. Schools need the owner of a local small business to adopt a classroom to help that teacher with supplies and provide regular volunteers to read to kids who are behind. Most companies could give employees one or two hours off a week or a month to volunteer at a local school, which would be a huge help for a teacher. Dads could give time to hang out in the hallway, at lunch, or on the playground. After you go the first time, text a couple of people that night and tell them to come help you next time, or challenge another small business to adopt the classroom next door. That's leadership that makes a difference. That's rebuilding the wall instead of complaining about it.

Thousands of years later, we still marvel at the faith and tenacity of Nehemiah. He faced real opposition, took on a challenge, and got it done. I encourage you to read the whole biblical story of Nehemiah. (It will take you less than half an hour to read it.) There are countless leadership principles contained in the ancient story—and I will mention a few more in the coming chapters of this book, because as you might recall, I am obsessed with his story. Nehemiah just kept doing something until it was done; then he kept going to do something else. You can plainly see in the final chapter, there was still more to be done in Jerusalem, but progress was made in the short time Nehemiah led the people. Something got done; something that made a difference.

EVERYTHING, SOMETHING, OR NOTHING

When we face a problem, we must determine whether we are going to do everything, something, or nothing. When the problem is small—like piled-up laundry in the corner of the room—everything can be solved in a day. Homelessness, racism, cultural anger, or mental health cannot be solved in a day, so we must choose to do "something" or "nothing." Even though the problem is overwhelming and nationwide, doing "something" affects a few people in a dramatic way, including your own family. Doing "nothing" just maintains the painful status quo.

Pray about a problem, then get to work doing something.

No one can cure cancer, Alzheimer's, or diabetes alone, but that doesn't mean that the millions of people who donate, serve their family, and work toward a cure aren't making a difference. They are doing what they can, where they are, to solve a huge issue. They have chosen to do "something" instead of sitting back and doing "nothing."

Don't just live in our cultural debris field and do nothing until everything can be fixed. Do something for someone and see what a difference it makes in that person and in you. That principle will work in a community, and it will work in Washington; we just have to apply it. Pray about a problem, then get to work doing something.

5

THE FOUNDATION

"When the foundations are being destroyed,
what can the righteous do?"

—PSALM 11:3

really don't know what made me think about it, but I couldn't get the story out of my cluttered mind one day. I don't even remember if I first heard the story in a math class or in a world history class, since I took them so long ago. For some reason, I thought about the challenge of Archimedes: "Give me a lever long enough and a fulcrum on which to place it, and I shall move the world." Even a United States Senator can say, that is some kind of ego.

Archimedes of Syracuse (the city in Sicily, not the one in New York) was born in 287 BC and died at the hands of the Romans in 212 BC. He was a true genius. He invented the Archimedes screw to raise water, created massive catapults to defend his town against the Romans, and wrote the definition of pi—the ratio of the circumference of any circle, regardless of the size of the circle, to the diameter of the circle equals approximately 3.14, or pi. (I always assumed he thought of that definition on March 14th.) He was gifted in every area of geometry, in other areas of mathematics, and in physics. Contrary to any movie depiction of Archimedes' grave, his tomb was inscribed with one of his favorite formulas, the ratio of a cylinder circumscribing a sphere. That is a true math nerd to the end.

When Archimedes' bold statement—about a place to stand and a lever long enough to move the world—randomly crossed my mind, I couldn't remember the exact quote. So, I did a quick search on it to refresh my memory. To my surprise, I found physics-obsessed folks (you know who you are) having an extensive online debate on how long the lever would have to be and how much force it would take to move the world. Apparently, over two millennia later, people are still trying to work out the formula on that lever. The intellectual math folks should talk to the intellectual English folks about the word "metaphor."

As I laughed about the physics and math debate online, I wondered if there was an online conversation about the stability of the fulcrum. In a quick search, I didn't find any interest there. Clearly, someone needs to do the math on the pressure and force of the lever on the fulcrum. If you are going to move the world with a lever, you'd better have a solid place to stand.

FOUNDATIONS MATTER

Early in our marriage, Cindy and I built a house together. Yes, we are still happily married. We hired a builder but did as many projects ourselves as we could to put some "sweat equity" into the house. On weekends and late nights, we painted, laid flooring, and even rolled out some of the insulation in the attic. We loved almost every part of the process. You can ask Cindy sometime about laying sod in the yard to find out quickly the part she really did *not* like. When I say she did not like rolling sod in the yard, I mean *really, really did not like.*

Seven months after we broke ground, we backed up the truck in the driveway to move our old stuff into our beautiful new house. Unfortunately, six months after move-in day, cracks in the walls also started moving in. By month seven, the oven would not close, and a pencil could roll across the kitchen countertop when you put it down. We had a beautiful house on a terrible foundation. The full story of what happened next needs a book of its own. Suffice it to say, we earned a graduate degree over the next three years in God's faithfulness and the importance of a strong foundation.

What you build on matters. In our case, we discovered the hard way that the lot we had bought and built the house on had been previously used as the dumping spot for the neighborhood during development. Under the solid-looking soil were more than eight feet of burnt, bulldozed trees, uncompacted fill dirt, and construction debris. It all looked fine, until you put a house on top of it; then everything under it started moving. Dirt looks solid, but when you add enough pressure, you find out if the layer underneath is as solid as what is on top.

There is a common belief that the pressure of Washington changes people after they are elected. After serving there for over a decade, I don't believe that is true. I think the pressure of Washington exposes in a person's life what was already under the surface. Members, staff, and interns all face unique pressure in the fishbowl of Washington. When the pressure is applied, their foundation is tested. Those who have a solid family, strong faith, and fixed values will handle the pressure differently from those who do not. It doesn't matter if you are headed to Congress, headed to a conference, or headed to college; the quality and strength of your foundation will always be exposed when pressure is applied.

WHAT AMERICA IS BUILT ON

Our American foundation is the United States Constitution. The Constitution is the oldest continuously operational codified constitution in the world. By the way, if you did not know it, that statement is a somewhat disputed fact. The micro-state of San Marino believes it has the oldest constitution because parts of it have existed since 1600. But not all of that constitution was written, so I don't think their constitution counts. Besides, with no disrespect to San Marino, there are more people in Muskogee, Oklahoma, than there are in San Marino. But I digress.

Our Constitution has been our legal foundation for two and half centuries. It can be amended but never surrendered. Our Constitution has been legally challenged thousands of times over our history, but it is still our foundation. Every time someone has proclaimed a "constitutional crisis" in our history, the Constitution has endured. On the contrary, Venezuela has had at least twenty-six constitutions (some say twenty-seven) since its founding in 1811. We have amended our Constitution as many times as Venezuela has written a whole new constitution.

Any challenges we face in government are not because our Constitution is weak or out of date. Our problems occur when we don't follow our Constitution. The endless executive orders, the regulatory chaos, and the unwillingness of Congress to do its job show our weaknesses, not the Constitution's.

When I was sworn into Congress, we had a formal dinner with all the new members of Congress and their families in the Rotunda for the Charters of Freedom at the National Archives. If you know your way around D.C., you already know that is the majestic room where the Constitution, the Declaration of Independence, and the Bill of Rights have been on permanent display since December 1952.

As a side note, before the current National Archives was dedicated, our official copy of the U.S. Constitution literally had no home for 163 years. It moved around multiple places and into a myriad of offices, vaults, buildings, and basements, including Fort Knox during World War II. It was moved around by train, covered wagon, a Model T, and a military transport.

Probably the most unique moment for the Constitution was during the War of 1812, when our founding documents were evacuated from Washington, D.C., before the British rudely burned the Capitol in August of 1814. The documents were hidden in a gristmill in Alexandria, Virginia, and then moved to an abandoned house in Leesburg, Virginia. Our historic documents were locked up in an empty house, and the key was given to a local pastor, Reverend John Littlejohn, who was also the sheriff and tax collector for Loudoun County. Pastor Littlejohn guarded the Constitution, the Declaration of Independence, and the Bill of Rights for two weeks, until they were moved back to Washington, D.C., after the British soldiers had left town. (Clearly, this was well before our current "Special Relationship" started with the British.)

While my family and I were seated at a formal dinner with the other new Members of Congress at the National Archives the night after our swearing into Congress, my 14-year-old daughter, Hannah, stared at the Constitution as she attempted to eat and said over and over, "It's right there; it's right there!" She probably said it fifteen times during our meal. We just replied, "Yes, it is right there." That evening, the weight of the task ahead of us was palpably heavy. The document in the glass case in front of us gave free people, for the first time in human history, the right to govern themselves in a way that would allow us to become the greatest nation in the history of the planet. With that gift, we also received the awesome responsibility to maintain that freedom.

The United States of America became the most powerful, moral, and generous nation in the history of the world because of our constitutionally guaranteed freedom and our distinct American spirit. We recognize our freedom comes from God and is guarded by our law and each generation's commitment to that law. We cherish our freedom.

However, a recent Pew Research study noted that for adults under thirty years old, 28 percent had a positive view of socialism and only 24 percent had a positive view of capitalism. Clearly, our nation is seeing the effect of leftist college professors, government teachers, and social media influencers who eagerly teach the next generation the "problems" of freedom and the benefits of socialism. However, before we blame others, we should remember that it is always the first responsibility of parents in each generation to reaffirm our foundational truths so the next generation will not fall for the lie. When adults constantly complain about our government and government leaders, the natural response from America's youth will be, "What type of government might work better?" The next generation needs to hear a clear and positive reaffirmation of our nation's foundational documents and values louder than our complaints about government leaders.

> *We recognize our freedom comes from God and is guarded by our law and each generation's commitment to that law.*

DECIDING YOUR OWN FOUNDATION

There is a growing belief that government can change a culture, for good or bad. I do not share that belief. You choose to live your values or reject them each day. Those in government can be a good or bad role model, and government can encourage or discourage certain behaviors. But your foundation is not from government; it is from your family, your faith, and your own choices. That means you cannot change culture by just electing new people in government or imposing new laws. If you try to reform culture by changing the government, you will find out just how resilient old habits can be.

Laws do not make us better people; our families and our churches make us better people. Laws and law enforcement just provide boundaries for the depravity we all have in our souls. When the family, churches, and nonprofits struggle or fail in their task, no amount of government can compensate. If you want a great example of this, just say the word "prohibition."

The abuse of alcohol in the nineteenth and early twentieth centuries led to widespread crime, family poverty, and countless accidents and incidents. As a result, millions of people across the country joined in the push to abolish liquor in America. After decades of work, thousands of volunteers, and relentless lobbying by the Women's Christian Temperance Union and the Anti-Saloon League, the House and the Senate approved a constitutional amendment on December 18, 1917. It was ratified by forty-six of the forty-eight states in just over a year—a record for an amendment—on January 16, 1919.

The Eighteenth Amendment to the Constitution stated, "After one year from the ratification of this article the manufacture, sale, or transportation of intoxicating liquors within, the importation thereof into, or the exportation thereof from the United States and all territory subject to the jurisdiction thereof for beverage purposes is hereby prohibited. The Congress and the several States shall have concurrent power to enforce this article by appropriate legislation . . ." That meant that starting in January 1920, "intoxicating liquors" would be illegal to manufacture, sell, or transport in America. Laws changed, and so the problem was solved, right?

When the Roaring Twenties began, officially alcohol use dropped dramatically, but speakeasies, bootleggers, and Al Capone rose quickly. Prohibition was the law of the land for only thirteen years. It was repealed by the Twenty-First Amendment on December 5, 1933, in the heart of the Great Depression. The law changed, but the values of individuals did not change.

As a funny aside, in my first campaign for Congress, a person once asked me to confirm I was not going to work for another prohibition. He knew I was a "teetotaler." (For those of you not from the south, that means I don't drink alcohol.) He was worried I would take up the crusade to ban alcohol again. I told him no for two reasons: First, prohibition did not work the first time, and second, I would lose the vote of a bunch of friends of mine from church.

While I am chasing a rabbit, it's interesting to me that Dry January, Sober October, and "mocktails" have become "a thing." More people are thinking through the cost of alcohol to their wallet, their family, and their body. Culture is starting to turn, ever so slightly, as people talk about the problems of excessive alcohol use instead of just swallowing the marketing and social media posts.

Outlawing alcohol in the 1920s did not stop its consumption or abuse, because it was a life choice with easy availability and no public accountability. Words on paper alone cannot change human behavior. We have clear laws that outlaw murder, but it has not stopped murder entirely—it has curtailed it, but not stopped it. That does not mean we should have no laws about murder, child porn, or illegal drugs; of course, we should. I just want to remind us that law and public consequences are only a single step in the journey to stop the destruction of our future, our families, or human life.

Every law has a moral foundation, but you cannot make someone moral by passing a law. Fixing culture with a law is as ineffective as prohibition. When you look at human history (or even the human present), it's not hard to see our depravity and our propensity to be selfish, violent, and arrogant. Voting to ban something seems simple, quick, and efficient, except the problem in culture will remain. Changing the law is not enough; we must change hearts and the person's foundation. We all have a job to do to reaffirm our national values.

A nation is built on its values, which are passed down through its families. When families are strong, the nation is strong. It is possible for values to drift, be destroyed, or be surrendered, but typically an individual's foundational values will be built by their family, maintained by their family, and passed on through their family. Families teach children a work ethic, values, character, sacrifice, and kindness. If children do not see or hear foundational values at home, they will search for someone or somewhere else to figure out a foundation on which to build their life, because everyone longs for a foundation.

When families pass on values like respect, hard work, and education, we strengthen the nation. But when families struggle, the nation struggles. One of the most significant things anyone could do for the future of our country is to be a role model for their own kids or grandkids and volunteer to help other kids in struggling families. The volunteers at our churches, schools, and nonprofits are true national heroes. When someone steps in to help a child establish a moral foundation and provide a safe place to learn and be loved, they dramatically change that child's future and the future of the nation. Mentors, pastors, teachers, Boys and Girls Clubs, YMCAs and YWCAs, after-school tutors, and thousands of other volunteers help kids every week in struggling families. They need our encouragement, time, and support.

> If children do not see or hear foundational values at home, they will search for someone or somewhere else to figure out a foundation on which to build their life, because everyone longs for a foundation.

Kids and families need role models, coaches, and friends, not just a check from government. When things are really hard, government is not there; people are there. I'm not saying the law or government doesn't have a role to play; both clearly do. But building character is a heart issue, not a legal issue.

In my childhood days, when it was just Mom and my brother, occasionally Mom would bring a newspaper to the table and read a news story. Then, she would challenge my brother to take one point of view on the issue, and I would have to take the other point of view in a full-on, dinner-long, table debate. As I reflect on those evenings at home, it's clear my mom worked to build foundational values in both of us. However, my mom might have known that my brother and I would argue at the table every night anyway. She might as well pick the topic for the fight.

She taught us how to think and how to think about others. Mom also kept a little plastic bread loaf on the table with paper scripture verses sticking out of the top. My brother and I would pull out one of the verses and read it out loud each night before we prayed over our meal. That "Bread of Life" and the dinner table debates on current events sparked my passion for God, people, and ideas. She laid a foundation.

I have a friend who does "Gramp Camp" for the grandkids each summer. All the grandkids come to their grandparents' house for a week, which allows my friend's married kids to have a week vacation without their kids. It is a good deal for everyone. Gramp Camp is carefully planned with activities every day for all the grandkids, which includes a couple of fun teaching times each day that are focused on passing on their faith and their family values. The grandparents are intentionally laying a foundation for their grandkids, instead of hoping they will pick up good values while they are scrolling on TikTok.

As I think about my bride, Cindy (which I do all time), it's obvious that our marriage has survived very stressful times because the foundation of our marriage was our commitment to God and each other. As we prepared for our wedding, Cindy suggested we write our own wedding vows and ring exchange instead of using the traditional vows. That was a great idea, but it was also a tough assignment for a twenty-four-year-old guy to think through how to articulate a lifelong marital commitment.

One of us, probably Cindy, but I honestly don't remember, came up with the idea to deepen the meaning of our wedding rings. My ring would not be a reminder of my commitment to Cindy, it would be a reminder of her commitment to me. When we exchanged rings, I started by saying, "This is a constant reminder of my commitment to you . . ." Cindy's ring reminds her each day, no matter where she is, whom she is around, or what happens, I am committed to our marriage.

When Cindy takes off her wedding ring to do a task around the house or get ready in the morning, I try to pick up the ring and slip it back on her beautiful finger, when she is ready, and say, "This is a constant reminder of my commitment to you." Our rings are symbols of our marriage's foundation.

As we build our life together, we also work to remember that God is the one who meets our every need. He is the strongest foundation. Cindy is an incredible wife, but she is a terrible god. When I expect Cindy to meet every need in my life, I put a demand on her that only God can fulfill.

MY SOLID FOUNDATION

I mentioned earlier that the life shift to politics was a complete interruption for our family. After more than two decades in youth ministry, no one, including us, saw the Senate on the horizon. In fact, depending on your relationship with a youth pastor at some point in your life, it may terrify you that a youth pastor is now in the United States Senate. To calm your trepidation, please know that I don't wear shorts to the office, serve pizza in the gym, have a marshmallow-eating contest in the cloakroom, or drive the van to pick up Senators each morning.

It is hard to describe the joy of serving students and families for more than twenty years. My wife and I walked with many students, parents, and student leaders through tough seasons of life in a culture that often despises our faith and our love for all people. Parenting is hard, but so is being a teenager. Students face indescribable pressure from friends around them and social media "influencers" to dress, speak, believe, date, try new drugs, or waste their life, just like them.

As a youth pastor, a significant portion of my job was speaking truth into teenagers who would allow me to challenge them, even after they ignored their parents. For some reason, with many students, I could say the exact same thing that their parents said, but they thought I was a genius, while their mom or dad was an idiot. By the way, I am confident that my daughters went through the same stages as they grew up, but this time I was the parent and someone else was the genius.

When you teach (or raise) teenagers, the clock is always ticking. The graduation deadline is always coming. To make sure I stayed focused on the priorities as a youth pastor, I broke down the foundational concepts into three big buckets: what did a student need to know (doctrines), be (character), or do (habits) to authentically walk with God and other people. When I outlined an intentional plan to help a child stand on a biblical foundation, it kept me focused on what mattered, instead of being distracted with what did not.

The joy of seeing the spiritual light come on in the eyes of a teenager who is struggling is a blessing. However, it is an even bigger blessing when you randomly run into those teenagers years later at a store and they tell you about their life, their family, and their continued spiritual growth. Serving students in ministry and

> *I respect the right of every person to live the faith of their choice, and I expect every person to also respect my right to live my faith, even as an elected official.*

serving families in the Senate are both products of the foundational truth in my life, my faith in Jesus.

I freely admit that there is no way to know the faith journey or perspective of every person reading this book. I cannot know how you will think or respond to my spiritual story because faith is intensely personal. Americans have the constitutionally protected right to have any faith of their choosing, change their faith, or have no faith at all. That is one of the many wonderful things about being an American, and it is one of the basic human rights that our nation should prioritize exporting around the world at every opportunity.

I respect the right of every person to live the faith of their choice, and I expect every person to also respect my right to live my faith, even as an elected official. I cannot and should not impose my faith on anyone, but I can live my faith, just like you can live yours.

One Sunday at church, when I was eight years old, I actually listened to my pastor, W. A. Criswell. If you know an eight-year-old boy, you know that is a miracle. Late that evening, I was still thinking about the basic truth that there is a God who loves me, but I did not know Him. That night, lying in my bed alone, I prayed and asked Jesus to forgive my sins and guide my life. It was not a complicated prayer (Did I mention, I was eight years old?), but it was the beginning of a lifelong relationship with God. It was the first stone of a new foundation.

Over the years, I never regretted that decision as a child, not once. Still today, I spend time reading scripture each morning and evening, and I pray multiple times throughout my day. I continue to preach at churches when invited, lead small-group Bible studies, and tell other people who are interested about how they could know the love of Jesus. My walk with Jesus has continued to grow, even in the swamp of Washington. Each week, I walk the Hart Senate Office Building and pray for the other Senators and their staff. Every Tuesday morning I eat breakfast with a group of seniors as we study the Bible together. We all need God's guidance.

Years ago, I was struck by several verses that challenged my daily walk with God in a new way. One was the simple, foundational description of God as "The Shepherd." I will admit, I like eating lamb chops, but I know very little about shepherds. One of the most familiar chapters in the Bible is Psalm 23, "The Lord is my shepherd, I lack nothing. He makes me lie down in green pastures, He leads me beside quiet waters, He refreshes my soul. He guides me along the right paths for His name's sake. Even though I walk through the darkest valley, I will fear no evil, for you are with me; your rod and your staff, they comfort me."

At almost every funeral I attend, the pastor reads Psalm 23. Even people who do not read the Bible are often familiar with the simple statement, "The Lord is my shepherd." But have you ever stopped to consider what it practically means in daily life to have God as your Shepherd?

Shepherds protect, provide, and guide. For some reason, I had no problem with God as my protector, or my provider, but for years, I had not thought enough about God as my guide. This concept gets even clearer when Jesus said to His disciples in John 10, "My sheep listen to my voice; I know them, and they follow me." Jesus was clear; His sheep would understand His voice and know how to follow Him.

When Jesus said, "Come follow me" over and over to the disciples, He was reminding them that He is the Good Shepherd. Following Him should be more than just following principles of love, forgiveness, and kindness. "Follow me" remains a personal invitation to a covenant relationship with the living God who cares about each person enough to have a good plan for their lives.

You may not know where you are going in the days ahead or what you will do, but you can decide today whom you are going to follow.

When I speak at high school graduations, I understand that exactly zero people came to hear the speaker, so I keep it short. I typically challenge the graduates to settle any broken relationships with their family (not that teenagers ever argue with their parents) and resolve one of the foundational life questions, "Whom are you going to follow?" You may not know where you are going in the days ahead or what you will do, but you can decide today whom you are going to follow. Deciding to follow the latest musician, writer, or social media influencer is very different from determining you are going to follow the God who made the universe. I settled the issue in my life years ago, I am going to follow Jesus. No turning back.

DRIVER'S ED

For all of us who survived the stress and trauma of driver's ed, let me pull out of the deep recesses of your mind a couple of basic tenets: "Keep your head on a swivel" and "You drive toward what you look at." As you drive around a curve at night, if your eyes focus on the white line on the outside edge of the curve, your wheels will start to veer toward that white line. If you look at the giant truck next to you, your hands will steer you toward the truck. You must focus your eyes where you want to go and keep your head on a swivel to always scan around your vehicle to watch for threats. It is tough to do both things at once, but it's essential for a good driver.

These basic principles are also true in our lives and community. If a person consumes news twenty-four hours a day, tracks every political gossip story, and knows the ins and outs of social media, but their family is distant and they make no difference in their community, then they drive toward what they are focused on. Voting and civic engagement are extremely important, but your family, local nonprofit, and church direct the future of the country. We must keep our eyes on where we need to go, while we still watch for the threats to our future.

If you want to make the foundation of the nation stronger, focus on what is important to drive your life toward what is essential.

PLEASE ALLOW ME A MOMENT TO BE BLUNT

We are so busy, we rarely even consider the foundation of our life. We just get through each day and hope it all turns out fine. The good thing about building a life is we get to pick today what we will build on tomorrow. Yesterday may have been a mess, but today you have the option to either build on yesterday's mess or start a new stable foundation for you and your family tomorrow.

If you are trying to change the world through politics, but you are ignoring your marriage, your kids, and your grandkids, you are building your life on a weak foundation. I have seen too many people in leadership lose their marriage and family because they walked away from their foundation. Your first task is to love your family and pass on the right values to them. No other task will be greater than that one, and no one is more qualified than you to do it. There is a reason one of the most critical passages of scripture in the Jewish and Christian faith is Deuteronomy 6:5-9: "Love the Lord your God with all your heart and with all your soul and with all your strength. These commandments that I give you today are to be on your hearts. Impress them on your children. Talk about them when you sit at home and when you walk along the road, when you lie down and when you get up. Tie them as symbols on your hands and bind them on your foreheads. Write them on the doorframes of your houses and on your gates."

A friend of mine posted in his house their family declaration. He and his wife sat for an evening and discussed the key values they wanted to pass down to their children, then they printed up the list and posted it. They talk about one of their values each week and remind each other that they are all trying to live out their family declaration. It sounds like Deuteronomy 6 in action. Intentionally living and passing down their foundational values.

Foundations of faith, patriotism, moral values, and excellence must be caught and taught. They absolutely can be passed down when we intentionally model those foundational truths. We won't be perfect, but we should strive for better. If we are going to help our nation with its turnaround, we need to make sure we are living on a solid foundation before we pick up Archimedes' lever and try to move the world.

6

BEES WILL KILL YOU

"I love mankind . . . it's people I can't stand!!"

—LINUS SPEAKING TO LUCY IN A 1959 PEANUTS CARTOON

"As a father has compassion on his children,
so the Lord has compassion on those who fear Him;
for He knows how we are formed,
He remembers that we are dust."

—PSALM 103:13-14

My daughter Jordan does not like bees. In fact, she freaks out over bees; always has. Yes, she has seen the social media reminders that bees are essential pollinators, and that the universe would experience catastrophic collapse without bees. But she still does not like the little thumb-sized airborne yellow-and-black predators. By the way, she is not alone. Pretty good chance you like honey, but you don't want one of the tiny honey manufacturers in your bedroom at night.

When Jordan was about twelve years old, our family was enjoying a small-town Oklahoma county fair together when I spotted a beekeeper's table. I thought this could be a perfect moment to allow Jordan to quiet her fears by asking questions of someone who makes a living hanging out with bees. The beekeeper seemed like a nice lady, with a pleasant smile and an interesting tabletop beehive display. As I turned toward the beekeeper, Jordan noticed the huge see-through plastic beehive on the table and curtly asked, "Dad, where are we going?" I calmly replied, "We are going to meet the beekeeper."

As I approached the table, I introduced myself and the cute redheaded girl beside me with the racing heartbeat and said, "My daughter is afraid of bees. I thought you could talk her through what you do and how safe bees really are." The beekeeper looked straight at Jordan and said, "Bees will kill you." I was suddenly in a moment of paternal shock and overwhelming regret, but like a deer in the headlights, I could not move before the beekeeper leaned closer to Jordan and said, "If you ever are attacked by bees, pull your shirt over your head, ignore all modesty, and run."

As the beekeeper spoke, she pounded her fist on the table for emphasis, which made the bees in the clear plastic hive aggressively buzz, which, of course, made the whole scene even more intense. However, she wasn't finished warning Jordan. She continued, "Be careful not to scream when you run. Bees always go for your throat. If you scream, the bees will fly into your open mouth and sting you in the throat." She pounded her fist again, adding, "Your throat will swell closed, and you will die. So don't scream; just run as fast as you can. Just run."

That is exactly what I wanted to do at that moment. Cindy, seeing the deepening pollinator trauma on Jordan's face, gently walked up and pulled Jordan away, leaving me awkwardly standing there to finish up the conversation with the worst exposure therapist on the planet. My great dad idea was an epic fireball of failure that has become legend in our family. Jordan is still afraid of bees, in fact even more so now. To this day, if I bring up an idea that is even slightly risky, someone in the family will say, "Pull your shirt over your head and run. But don't scream; just run."

It seemed like such a good idea at the time. I clearly needed to go back to dad school and study more.

We all want things to turn out perfect every time, but we all know they don't. We mess up. No doubt about it. Our communities need help, but we sometimes think they need help from someone better than me. Our imperfections cause us to sit back and do nothing when the people around us need a humble, imperfect, servant leader. Somebody to do something. Even if they don't get it right every time. Frankly, anyone who is willing to serve is better than someone who is highly qualified but unwilling to serve.

We shouldn't allow our past mistakes, imperfections, and weaknesses to keep us from serving our family, our community, and our nation. We also shouldn't set an unrealistic standard of perfection for leaders. As Psalm 103:13-14 says, "As a father has compassion on his children, so the Lord has compassion on those who fear Him; for He knows how we are formed, He remembers that we are dust."

I AM NOT PERFECT, AND I PROVE IT EVERY DAY

I'm not a perfect dad or a perfect leader. Everyone makes mistakes, but my mistakes get posted online and shared thousands of times. Of course, even when I don't make a mistake, someone online will just make up a mistake for me and post it. The whole world seems to enjoy celebrating the imperfections of anyone in public life. I promise, I see the plank in my own eye. Thankfully, for my sake, perfection is not required for service or leadership. That fact is obvious, based on the current makeup of Congress.

Our Founding Fathers didn't have any delusions about their own perfection or of the perfection of the people around them. Remember from an earlier chapter Gouverneur Morris, the author of the phrase "We the People"? He once wrote in his diary, "Every Day of my Life gives me Reason to question my own Infallibility." Famously, our second President, John Adams, once said, "If all men were angels, we would not need government." The founders recognized the depravity of mankind and understood that power was best defused and determined by the decisions of "we," not the dominance of a fallible authoritarian "they."

Congress has issues because members of Congress are fallible people. To compensate for our personal weaknesses, our Constitution empowers every voice and opinion to help decide an issue so we can chip away our individual faults to demonstrate our common insight and imperfections. If everyone sits back and waits for someone else to engage, we end up where we have ended up.

Leaders need your ideas, friendship, and support. When people stop me and ask how they can pray for me, I'm always grateful and encouraged because I know I need God's help to serve so many people. I also know I do not know the answer to every question in the universe. When you pray for leaders, I encourage you to ask God to protect their family, give them wisdom in their decisions, and give them the discernment to know what to do and what not to do. When we pray, God directs and empowers us in ways we will never understand this side of heaven. When a friend gives you genuine encouragement, constructive criticism, or a prayer on the spot, it's a gift. Blessing imperfect leaders makes them better. Cursing imperfect leaders makes them bitter.

I freely admit that I have been over my head hundreds of times as we started debating an issue facing our nation. It may surprise you to know that I do not have decades of experience in international tax policy, high voltage electricity transmission, satellite defense systems, the national airspace, artificial intelligence, foreign terrorist threats, or quantum physics. It's entirely possible that you do not have experience in all those issues either, but decisions need to be made.

I'm the one in the chair on behalf of my great state, even in my inadequacy, which means I need to learn the details, do the work, and make the best decision possible on the tough issues. That is true for any person in the Senate, any small business owner, any parent, and anyone else in leadership. None of us knows or has done everything. Leaders are not omniscient. But true leaders should be committed to study and do the work to become educated on each issue. People are counting on them to do it right.

I have cast thousands of votes in more than a decade of serving the nation in Congress. Most of them I would never change, but some of them I would go back and switch if I could. There are people I trusted in Congress early on but later learned I should trust less and verify more. Over the years, I have given some angry and divisive floor speeches, instead of bringing solutions and common-sense direction. I still don't balance my time well. Sometimes, I literally ignore my own advice. If anyone tells you that they always get it right, they need to watch a recording of their life in slow motion, so they have an opportunity to count their issues, starting with pride and arrogance.

> *My history teaches me that I can learn, grow, and change, and so can you.*

I have a history, and so do you, and so does our nation. My history teaches me that I can learn, grow, and change, and so can you. My personal history doesn't make me damaged goods; it makes me grateful for the forgiveness of Jesus. I absolutely believe any person can experience the same grace and fresh start I experienced. Admitting I make mistakes should not prevent me from serving other people; it should allow me to lead with great compassion people like me who also make mistakes. To be clear, I was a sinner long before I was a Senator.

THE SPLINTER

Jesus had a funny carpenter story (yes, Jesus had a sense of humor) about a man who tried to help his neighbor get a tiny wooden splinter out of his eye, which was very kind of the man since splinters certainly hurt, especially in your eye. However, the helpful man struggled because he had a huge board sticking out of his own eye. The man was so focused on the problems of others, he refused to acknowledge that he had giant problems of his own.

As is typical for Jesus, the story is not about a wooden plank sticking out of your eye; it's about acknowledging that we each need to work on ourselves. Jesus was not telling us to ignore the problems of others; He was telling us to first work on our own challenges and then help others. Maybe we just assume the plank in our eye is fine, righteous, even fashionable; they just need to clean up "their act." I'm fine; "they" are the problem, right?

For the future of the nation, we need more people who are willing to serve, willing to learn, and willing to be the best role model possible to those behind them. More parents running for school board, more dads volunteering at their child's events, more families volunteering their time at a food bank, and more help for community events. Even if you don't know everything and you aren't perfect, people need your help. But to improve our leadership, we should not ignore our own imperfections.

We should humbly work on improving our attitude, habits and example, then keep serving.

I want to read more, exercise more, ask more questions, listen closer to people whom I disagree with, and a million other things to improve my service to my family and my nation. My road to more wisdom, more humility, and more strength to serve starts with admitting I do not know everything or do everything, but I have been forgiven by God and I have a new day to choose to get started serving.

When I am loading a truck to move, a moving company would be great, but I am grateful to just have a friend with a pickup and strong back. Some help is so much better than no help. Other people are imperfect, just like me. ("Inadequate" sounds better than "imperfect," but both would be true for most days.) When we feel we don't have enough time, resources, or expertise to help or lead, we need to acknowledge that things still need to get done, so let's get started anyway. Our nation needs more people who admit they are imperfect, even display their imperfections, but they are at least willing to help. Not every leader is a role model, but at least they were willing to do something for someone.

Your past mess may be exactly the message that others need to hear to persuade them to walk away from their own mess to have their own message.

Perfection is a great goal, even a godly goal, but we should all admit it's not possible in a world crammed full of selfishness and sin. It's always easier to tell yourself that you could never be a role model because of all you have done in your past, which lets you off the hook to ever lead or live better. It also ignores the power of God's forgiveness and the impact of a great story of redemption. Your past mess may be exactly the message that others need to hear to persuade them to walk away from their own mess to have their own message. Your past shouldn't be an excuse to do nothing, it should be a calling and a reminder that people need your help to not make the same mistakes you did. Take the risk: Serve imperfectly the imperfect people around you.

ROOKIES MAKE ROOKIE MISTAKES

On my first day as a new member of Congress, I was asked by the *New York Times* if they could shadow me for the day. They had selected a few new members, with no political background, to write a feature story about the unpolished "Tea Party" class coming into Congress in 2011. Of course, we were unpolished— in fact, still are. That year, a high percentage of the class had no election experience, including myself. The *New York Times* reporter was very professional but was also clearly experienced and comfortable around the Capitol offices. She watched me reading signs in the hallway to figure out which way to go to the meeting rooms, and she was there when I did my first TV interview in the Cannon House Office Building rotunda.

Television interviews look very different from the other end of the camera. Most of the time, you talk into the lens of the camera and listen to the questions through a clear plastic tube with an earpiece that is occasionally still warm from the last person who used it a few minutes ago. That day, I walked to the Rotunda and scanned across the Members of Congress, reporters, and camera operators to find my designated station for the interview in the Cannon building. When I found my spot, there was a camera on a tripod, a camera operator, and a chair with a corded microphone and earpiece sitting on it.

The camera operator (videographer to be precise) helped me put the earpiece in and connected the microphone to my suit jacket. Once I was wired up, I promptly sat down in the chair in front of the camera to await my interview. The camera operator patiently told me that this type of interview is called a "stand-up interview" for a reason and that the chair was only there to lay the microphone and earpiece between interviews. Of course, when the *New York Times* interview was released, it

> *Being perfect at doing nothing is not an admired skill.*

described in detail the moment when I tried to sit down for my first stand-up interview. Rookie mistake.

I wish I could tell you that was my last rookie mistake or that I have discovered a way to avoid rookie mistakes; I haven't. Rookies make rookie mistakes; that is just the way it is. I hate being a rookie at anything because I know there is no way around mistakes the first time you try anything. The only thing worse than a rookie mistake is never trying anything new. Being perfect at doing nothing is not an admired skill.

If you read leadership books, you will see a wide variety of opinions about how long it takes to become good at something. Some say 20 hours; some say 100 hours; others say 10,000 hours. But no one says you will be your best the first time you try something new. First things are hard and are rarely done well. We always joked with our older daughter that she was our practice round for parenting, which actually was not a joke, but don't tell her. Like every other parent, we had no idea what we were doing most of the time. We prayed, loved, and put her in the best situation we knew how, because every day was a new challenge. We were rookie parents.

No one is good at everything, especially the first time. Going to a new city, driving a different car, or even going to a church for the first time can be intimidating. However, when you make the decision to do a new thing, you make the decision to prepare yourself for the next great new thing. But first, you must conquer your fear of being a rookie and admit you will do rookie things your whole life, so you might as well learn how to be a rookie leader now.

Rookie leaders never get better at leading if they don't get past the first set of rookie mistakes. Don't beat yourself up over it; just apologize, learn from it, and keep going. Humility is a fantastic characteristic of true leadership. You took the risk to serve people and solve problems. The whole country is cheering you on, mistakes and all, because we need more people to serve and you chose to do it. Find a mentor, ask questions, and keep serving. Don't let the false image of social media convince you that everyone is cute and perfect. Our nation needs you to do something to help someone.

When you serve in the United States Senate, you see a cornucopia of new troubles every day. At any given moment, there is a crisis brewing in foreign policy, national defense, immigration, the economy, agriculture, small business, banking, education, energy, tax, rogue agencies, and a million other issues. It is overwhelming because the issues are different every day, people are counting on you to figure out which way to go on the new issue, and there is always a crowd of naysayers waiting to criticize your decision if it goes wrong. When Oklahomans ask me how they can help me, I almost always ask them to share their ideas and insights. I am not ashamed to ask for help from people who live the issues each day. We need fresh ideas, but we also should pursue the insights of people who have been around the block a few times to help us avoid some common mistakes.

My first year in the House of Representatives, I knew I needed some help. I was grateful to connect with an experienced Congressman named Mike Pence from Indiana, who chose to intentionally mentor a few new Congressmen each year. He was a Christian leader, a husband, a dad, and a former conservative talk radio host who had run for Congress. He was a safe person to ask the dumb questions and get some history on the issues we debated. He left the U.S. House a couple years after I got there to do a couple other impressive things for Indiana and our nation. I bring him up because everyone in leadership, even in Congress, needs someone to help them through the rookie mistakes.

> *Learning from the mistakes of others is free; learning from your own mistakes is expensive.*

If you have been in leadership for any period of time, in any role, there are probably many who could benefit from your wisdom. You learned from the mistakes you made the first time you led. They need someone to help them through the first mistakes they will make. Learning from the mistakes of others is free; learning from your own mistakes is expensive.

When you mentor someone on a project or task, you train new leaders on the job and multiply the passion for the solution. You recognize that the world is not dependent on you and the task is bigger than you. Leadership is not doing everything;

it's inviting others to do the work with you. You may carry the vision, but if you don't share the workload and raise up more leaders around you for the future, your vision will die a very weary death. Leadership can make you bitter, broken, and beat.

If you are a person who thinks you must lead everything because other people will not get it right, you may need people around you to help you stop trying to run the world. Many nonprofit organizations and churches will tell you about the 90/10 rule for volunteers. Ninety percent of the work is done by 10 percent of the volunteers, leading to burnout and distraction. It's likely some of you reading this chapter think you're not doing enough, when you are already stretched finer than a frog's hair split three ways. (I have no idea what that really means, but a friend of mine has said it for years, and it sounds really thin.)

Add new people to the task. In the future, they could change the nation in ways you could never measure. There are students who are ready to conquer the world, moms who have a passion for our community, retired folks who suddenly have time and wisdom to share, and millions of others who would lead in small or large ways, if only someone would directly ask them to help. Sure, they are rookies, and they will make rookie mistakes, but so did you when you started leading. Intentionally mentor the next generation of wise leaders; our nation needs them.

On the other end of the spectrum, there is a certain pull in life toward sitting down, the old habit, status quo. It's tough to do something the first time or the first time in a long time. If you have a consistent habit of serving others in practical ways and people to serve alongside, it is easier to keep serving. If you don't have a place to serve or a group of people you regularly serve with, the pull of the couch is strong. Binge-watching the latest series is so much easier than mentoring a child down the street or volunteering the first time for a nonprofit.

If you want to awaken a nation, change a culture, and right the wrongs, you need to get off the couch and get started. Then you need to add some people beside you, even if they are rookies. Maybe, especially if they are rookies. Ask someone to help, they may say yes and change the world with you.

7

CALLING

"If you don't know where you are going,
any road can take you there."

—GEORGE HARRISON, "ANY ROAD"

"Calling" is a scary word; it sounds so mystical or super-spiritual. "Calling" conjures visions of burning bushes, terrifying angels, and booming voices from heaven. Some use the word "calling" carefully, for fear of being misunderstood or dismissed. Understandably so. You may be surprised to know that many Senators in private conversations talk openly about their own calling to come to Congress. I have not heard anyone share a vision of a burning bush, but I have heard multiple Senators talk about a burning passion that would not leave them until they prayed and acted on it. They even call it "a calling" in private but hesitate to say so in public because it sounds way too spiritual.

Except *calling* is not *crazy*; it's normal. It's a unique and overwhelming sense of obligation to serve people in a specific way. It's the thought you can't stop talking about and can't stop thinking about that drives you to get up in the morning, but probably drives the people around you crazy. Calling sounds like what Nehemiah experienced. He heard about a problem that he could not stop thinking and praying about, so he acted on it. For some unknown reason, that seems reasonable for someone in stories from long ago, but not now and not for someone "like me." To make this clearer, a career is what you do for a living. A calling is what you do because you are living. A career is what you are paid for. A calling is what you were made for.

I did not anticipate running for the United States Congress. In fact, it was never on our family radar. No one has ever said to a youth pastor, "You should be a U.S. Senator." No one in my family was in politics; we had no special connections, or money. I didn't even run for student council in high school. I was a husband, a dad, and an informed voter. But in 2008 and 2009, my bride, Cindy, and I both sensed clearly that God was calling us to leave the ministry that we loved in order to dive into the political maelstrom. I could never adequately explain what a huge change that was in our lives.

> *A career is what you are paid for. A calling is what you were made for.*

We could not shake the calling. We prayed about it for months, wrestling with what that would mean for our family and our careers. We shared the story with people we trusted who would pray for us and with us. We listened for God's direction, and we honestly hoped this was all a distraction, not a calling. But it was a calling; it would not go away.

God did not speak to us audibly. There were no words written in the clouds over our heads. No angel appeared to us in a dream. It was just an overwhelming sense that we were supposed to run for Congress, right now, for a specific seat and to trust that God knows what He is doing. In the end, I had a simple decision to make: Was I going to follow my calling or ignore it? I remember saying to Cindy as we left church one Sunday in March of 2009, "I'm going to be an old man one day, telling my grandchildren about the time I didn't follow God if we don't step into this race." I could not stop reflecting on a moment years before when I had met a man in his eighties who had privately told me about a time in his twenties when he had heard

God's call on his life, but he had been afraid to trust God's plan. Literally decades later, he still had deep regret and a seemingly endless stack of "what-ifs." I never want to be that person. When you hear God's call, you know it. It never leaves you.

So, after we finished camp that summer, I resigned my position and announced I was running for Congress. September 1, 2009, was a normal day for most people, but for the Lankford household, it was life revolution day. Since I served in a non-profit, I chose to resign rather than put the ministry at risk or give it any political attention.

I believe the church should prioritize reaching all people from all backgrounds, from all political perspectives, every week. While every pastor should boldly speak the truth in love from scripture on any topic, when a church becomes aligned with a political party, it sends a false message to half of the community, who are not from that political party, that they are not welcome at the cross. Which, of course, is false, even heretical. A church that is actually a political operation is distracted from its primary mission to help people personally experience the love and grace of God. There are thousands of places where political topics are discussed every week, but there is only one place where the message of Jesus' love and forgiveness is discussed every week: the church.

For the next year, I campaigned full-time. Cindy worked longer hours as a very talented speech language pathologist, and we lived off our life savings, which as you can imagine, since I had been a youth pastor, was not significant. Most of our friends were initially shocked, but then pleasantly surprised. We were thankfully never alone on the journey. Literally, from the first day, I had friends contact me and make incredible life sacrifices to join us.

As I shared our story and commitment, others sensed their own calling to join us as volunteers. They put their family and their finances on the line, just like we did. I cannot begin to describe how humbling and affirming it was to take a first step on a terrifying journey of faith and to immediately be joined by people who also chose to trust the calling of God in their life. None of us had any assurances that this would work, but we all knew it was right. It was "We the People."

Of course, there were also friends who had been actively partnered with us in ministry for years who were not too sure about us leaving "the ministry" for politics, since politics is such a "dirty business." I heard over and over some version of "Washington, D.C., is a modern-day Sodom and Gomorrah that we should condemn, not join." All I could say to them was, politics will remain a dirty business until more good people follow God's call anywhere. Besides, at the end of Sodom and Gomorrah, God was pulling people out, not calling people in. If God had not written off D.C., why should I?

A passage like Romans 13:6, reminds us that government is in God's eye when it states, " . . . the authorities are God's servants, who give their full time to governing." America is not a theocracy; we are a representative Republic. I am not a Christian nationalist, but I am a Christian who is serving the nation. People of faith are also citizens of our Republic who should be represented just like everyone else. Without question, the biblical ethics our nation was founded on will fade out of the conversation of government if people with a biblical worldview are intimidated out of running or just fail to engage in campaigns and as candidates. Government is open to everyone because our nation is open to everyone, but decisions are made in government by the citizens who run for office and win.

The campaign year of 2010 was a blur and needs a book of its own. Campaigns are essentially job interviews, very long job interviews. Each person decides on Election Day whom they want to hire for each task from the list of people who have submitted their applications. We had no money and no political connections, but we knew approximately how many people would vote, based on the number of people who had voted during the last primary election. So, our target was to earn the trust of more than half of the number of people who would vote in the next primary election. Each election really comes down to math.

Our family and a small group of volunteers worked every week for a year to meet people and ask for their vote. We identified the four key voting precincts that we had to win, and Cindy personally knocked on every door in those precincts. Did I mention that the summer of 2010 was a particularly hot summer?

While Cindy was going door to door, I worked every day to meet as many people as possible in small home meetings, at the mall, in coffee shops, or at community events. Each day, we would work to connect with new people. Every night, I researched conservative solutions to the issues our nation faced. Our family believed losing the election would not be the worst thing; winning the election and being unprepared for the task would be the worst thing. I didn't want to be good at the job interview but terrible at the job. Unfortunately, some people seem to love campaigns more than the job, but that conversation will have to wait for another day.

Any large task needs determined partners to finish well. I don't always remember that truth. Each time I jump into a task alone and it fails, I'm reminded again that leaders need partners; in fact, true leadership demands it. The friends who jumped into the deep end of the pool with me during the 2010 campaign sacrificed incredible amounts of time. Terri, Bob, Holly, Greg, Neva, Patti, Sarah, Kaleb, Will, Kristen, Casey, Paul, Glenn, Steve, Heather, Brian, Frank, Gene, Jo, Stephen, Nick, and countless others made the difference. Those names may not mean anything to you, but they are all friends and "fellow called." If any one of them had not been there, there would have been a different result in the 2010 election. I can say that fact with confidence because we won the seven-person primary election in 2010 by only 1 percent.

The volunteers who joined us on the campaign journey were there because they also heard a calling to do something. They did what they could, where they could, and they made a difference for a bigger purpose. We should just sit down over a tall glass of sweet tea and talk about the first race sometime, so I could give you the bigger picture of what happens when a committed group of people faithfully serve their neighbors.

> *They did what they could, where they could, and they made a difference for a bigger purpose.*

After the election in November, the whole family flew to Washington for orientation. Yes, freshman members of Congress go through orientation, but no hazing rituals. There were ninety-seven newly elected, and very eager, House members that year. It was a remarkable group of leaders including Mike Pompeo, Tim Scott, Trey Gowdy, Kristi Noem, Sean Duffy, Reid Ribble, Todd Young, Mick Mulvaney, Cory Gardner, Jeff Landry, Vicky Hartzler, Billy Long, Ben Quayle,

Larry Bucshon, Tim Walberg, Andy Harris, Steve Womack, and many others.

DAY ONE

It's hard to describe the emotion of walking onto the floor of the United States Congress as a member for the first time. Awe-inspiring. Intimidating. Humbling. Elections are drama, stress, and chasing the unknown every day. Day one on the floor of the House of Representatives was a different level of drama and stress.

I walked alone through the wooden side door of the U.S. House Chamber to prepare for the swearing-in of the 112th Congress of the United States on January 3, 2011. I went early that day to stand there for a moment to get my bearings. Years before, I had sat in the gallery as a high school student on a Close Up trip, but this time I was on the floor taking an oath. This was not someone else's task; it was mine. I had the job of working with 434 strangers from around the country to get something done. Just for fun, I often encourage people to try to make a detailed decision about anything with over 400 equals; it is harder than it looks.

Raising your right hand to take the oath is like lifting a box of dishes when you are moving; it's heavy, and you know that there is a significant price if you drop it. In some way, I expected that emotion on day one. What I did not anticipate enough was the moment when I stood at Ronald Reagan Washington National Airport and watched my beautiful wife and daughters walk through TSA after the swearing-in ceremony. They were flying back home, and I was staying in Washington to work.

We stood on opposite sides of the security checkpoint staring at each other uncontrollably weeping. It was a shoulders-shaking, hot-face, snot-nosed, can't-make-it-stop, ugly cry. The cost of the task landed on our family simultaneously as our new reality of living half our year in separate time zones hit us.

There is always a cost to fix a problem. Small or large, if the problem could be fixed with no cost, it would have already been fixed.

The second cost of the task greeted Cindy and our daughters when they arrived at home—our hot-water tank had gone out in the freezing January temperatures while we were at orientation. Perfect timing.

All four of us prayed about running for Congress, and all four of us agreed this was our family calling. More about that in a moment. As simple as it sounds, we decided first what was right; then we determined we were going to do what was right, even if it had a cost. The right thing to do often has a very high price, but it is still right. The wrong thing always has a higher price, we just forget that sometimes until we have to pay it.

There is always a cost to fix a problem. Small or large, if the problem could be fixed with no cost, it would have already been fixed. When a problem remains, it's because people have determined that they are not willing to pay the price to fix it. Ignoring a problem simply means we think someone else should solve the problem, not us. They should sacrifice, not me.

This is true in an individual, family, neighborhood, state, or nation. Improving our mind, health, relationships, or faith all have a cost. In our hearts, we know we should do something to serve others and ourselves, but it is hard to pay the price of the first step. I learned early, if you notice a problem, you get to solve it. Maybe it was the people I was around, but if you ever mentioned a problem that you saw, you had to be the one to fix it. My mom was the queen of assigning tasks to the person who saw the problem.

The men who signed the Declaration of Independence understood well the cost of freedom in July of 1776. After they declared that they were separate from the British Crown, free and independent, they wrote the final sentence and signed the statement, "And for the support of this Declaration, with a firm reliance on the protection of divine Providence, we mutually pledge to each other our Lives, our Fortunes and our sacred Honor." As you probably know, many of them did sacrifice, significantly. We are the beneficiaries of the fruits of those sacrifices that several of them would not live to see.

> *The real question is: Are we willing to pay the cost of our calling to make a difference in our family, our community, and our nation?*

Your time, your finances, your reputation, and your heart are all at risk when you choose to serve people in a way that honors God and changes the future of the country. Nothing gets better by apathy; someone must stand out and set a new and better direction. The question is not if our calling will have a cost; we all know it will. Calling always has risk and a cost. The real question is: Are we willing to pay the cost of our calling to make a difference in our family, our community, and our nation?

Nothing changes until someone decides to pay the price to change it.

BACK TO THE ANCIENT

Calling is not about you or your title. Calling is about the God who calls us and the task he sets in front of us for a certain season of time. You may have noticed that the expendable servant Nehemiah was not looking for a new task when God called him. He was being faithful when God called him to a new task unexpectedly, but clearly. He just had to decide if he was going to ignore the calling or take it on.

In tough days, Nehemiah could always go back to the calling to serve the people of Jerusalem. Nehemiah believed that God was strong enough to complete the task and to call others to help, just like he was called. When the Senate gets noisy, angry, even childish, I remember that God called me for a season to serve in this place for a task according to his plan and purpose. I trust in a sovereign God who has a plan for each of us and all of us.

There are so many roles that need to be filled in our great nation right now. To paraphrase Jesus in John 4, the fields are ready, but the laborers are way too few. Pray for more people to step up to serve. This nation needs people who are willing to listen to God's leadership and do the task that he has set in front of us to do, no matter the role or title. Communities with poverty, homelessness, kids living without a role model, people struggling with addiction, seniors who need food assistance, volunteers for pregnancy resource centers, schoolteachers who need a volunteer aide, school board members, city councils, district attorney's offices, county clerks, and many more places all need someone who has a calling to serve and a willingness to love people.

We should not shy away from a calling because it seems big or hard. Sometimes it takes decades, and sometimes impossible things happen at impossible speeds. In the text of the story, Nehemiah heard about the problem in Jerusalem, prayed about it for four months, and then was on his way to Jerusalem a few months later. When he got there, the walls were rebuilt in less than two months. That is fast.

According to the timeline in the Book of Nehemiah, it was approximately ten months from his conversation with Hanani until the walls were rebuilt. That is the equivalent of two semesters at school for his whole life to change. If you want to narrow to the actual construction, it took fifty-two days—that is less time than it takes to grow and harvest a stalk of wheat. You could have your car in the shop longer than fifty-two days. He went from being a slave cup bearer to leading a nation out of poverty and danger in less time than some people go between getting a haircut. To put it in American holiday terms, he was a slave hundreds of miles away on Valentine's Day, but by Thanksgiving, the walls of Jerusalem were finished. He saw the problem, prayed, and then got to work.

To be fair, most problems are not solved in ten months. But to be frank, many problems have no one working on them, so we would never know if they could be solved in ten months. As you sit today, what problem is on your heart to work on that you have not started because you were too afraid, too tired, or just too busy to begin? Some challenges take years; ask the Shaws at Pocket Full of Hope in North Tulsa about mentoring and leading for decades. But some problems just need a leader to get started so they can get finished. It could be that your family, your work, or your community could experience a breakthrough if only someone would pray until God gave them a plan and then would get to work on that plan. If you are faithful to the calling, other people will be there when you take the first step. By this time next year, your life and the life of the people around you could be radically different, if you will get started.

Don't miss the other big point of the ancient story—Nehemiah was a slave, a cup bearer, living in another country, with no engineering or governing experience. God equipped him to save Jerusalem by leading the people of Jerusalem to repair their wall and help the nation's economy get back on track. (We don't have time for all he did for their debt, but trust me, it was significant.) When he started, he had no title, no money, and no experience. He saw the problem, prayed, and then got to work. God called him, equipped him for the calling, and raised up other people to help.

Your issue will never be that you don't have or know enough or that you aren't enough. If the problem is on your heart, you already have the first thing you need to get it done, your calling. You just must fight the pull of gravity to get off your couch and banish the false emotion that you are not the right person to lead. Remember, the right person to lead is the one who will get up and try. Most people won't try to make a difference, so if you will, you are the leader we need.

> *If the problem is on your heart, you already have the first thing you need to get it done, your calling.*

Where is the mess that you see that other people ignore, but you can't stop thinking about? There is a reason that God put that issue or problem on your heart. God gave you eyes to see it. Now you must decide if you are going to be Hanani, who griped and walked away, or Nehemiah, who prayed and went to work.

You will answer that question within days of reading this chapter by either ignoring the problems around you or getting on your knees and asking God, "What can I do to make a difference?" Which problem around you is your mission or your mess? You can't do everything, but you can do something. The worst option is to do nothing.

TALENTS

Jesus loved to drive home a truth with a story. In Matthew 25, He told a story about a rich guy who went on a long journey, but before he left, he gave three of his servants a unique opportunity. To one of his servants, he gave five bags of gold; to another, two bags of gold; and to the last, one bag of gold. Bags of gold were a huge responsibility, but it's clear from the story that the rich man considered each of his servants capable of investing his money and getting a return for what they had been given.

When the man returned from his trip, the one with five bags of gold returned double what he had been given. The servant who had two bags of gold also returned double what he had been given. But the servant with one bag of gold dropped a muddy bag of gold on the man's desk because he had literally buried the bag in the ground to protect it. As you could imagine, the rich guy was not happy with the third servant—for a multitude of reasons.

The story was not about the value of investing, compounding interest, or buried treasure. In the story, God is the one who sees the potential in you, and we are the servants who have God's talents and time for a purpose. Some have more talents and time than others, but the point of the story in Matthew 25 is the faithfulness of each person with what he had been given.

You may feel like you are the person with only a little bit of talent and a little bit of time. If so, you must decide if you will do nothing to serve people around you because your task is not "big enough" or public enough. Or you could be one of the other two people in the story who had great abilities from God, and you must daily determine if those gifts are going to be used to serve yourself or others. Your gifts, wealth, and talents were given to you by God to bless others; you should not squander them on yourself. When much is given, much is required.

I have a friend who is spending his retirement years working with the homeless, literally walking with people through their toughest days. I have another respected friend who asked the staff at his church, "What is the one volunteer job at our church that no one wants to do?" When they told him, he said, "Sign me up." Now every weekend, he sets up chairs, cleans the auditorium, and puts out drinks and snacks for the people coming each week. They found practical ways to serve people. They did not bury their talent in the ground; they determined they could do something to help someone. So they did. They are leading by serving. They shifted their life focus from personal success to eternal significance.

8

ANGRIER TODAY THAN YESTERDAY . . .

Dorothy: "How can you talk if you haven't got a brain?"

Scarecrow: "I don't know, but some people without brains do an awful lot of talking, don't they?"

—THE WIZARD OF OZ

The Senate cloakroom is a narrow L-shaped private room connected to the Senate floor with some well-worn, out-of-date furniture from the 1990s, a small table, decades-old wooden phone booths, and a few remarkable and very patient staff who manage the day-to-day operation of the Senate floor. For more than a century, that room has been the place where significant decisions are made that affect the direction of domestic and international policy. I have been in many serious conversations in that room. It's at times the actual "room where it happens."

Between votes not long ago, five of us were privately debating in the cloakroom one of the most consequential issues of our day—college conference realignment and the college football transfer portal. Both are quite possibly the worst things in college football history. The ability for a player to transfer to any school every year makes eighteen-year-old athletes free agents and teams just a gathering of temporary players. Conference realignment ruins historic rivalries all over America. We all have certain teams we like to cheer for and cheer against, and no one should mess with those games. Of course, the national debt, unequal justice, threats of terrorism, and high inflation are huge issues, but in the fall, the major driver of our national outrage has become conference realignment and the transfer portal.

Every day, there seems to be a new reason to be angry in the greatest country in the world. Social media, twenty-four-hour news, podcasts, and talk shows often work to keep us angry, so we will listen for the next crazy thing coming. Each day, media implies that if you are a real patriotic American, you should be angrier today than you were yesterday because the issue today is even worse than yesterday's angry issue. Of course, then they say the issue tomorrow may be even worse, so keep tuning in to find out.

There is no shortage of legitimate issues that make us angry. But I haven't met anyone who says they make their best decisions when they are angry. The University of Michigan's Center for Political Studies released a study on anger and cynicism in politics and its possible connection to social media use. They noted: "Emotions like anxiety and anger can drive people to the polls, motivate advocacy, and get people to seek and think more deeply about political information. But relentless negativity about the state of a country 'under threat' can also make people frustrated, disgruntled, and disengaged. Anger can affect our ability to see things as they are and make measured decisions that are important in a democracy." In layman's terms, anger can motivate us to action or make us do something dumb.

When you are elected to the House or Senate, you quickly run into a problem: You are one of 535 on Capitol Hill. How do you stand out in the crowd? The easy answer is: the same way to stand out in any crowd—do something that gets noticed. Wear something different, be the loudest, be first, be obnoxious, get a crazy haircut, be the most critical, or be the kindest. Of course, the preferred method to stand out in D.C. is always to be the angriest.

If you just want to be noticed in a crowd, anger is not a bad strategy. During a football game, the angry player on the sideline screaming at his teammates always gets some extra camera time. When there is a protest on the street, the media focuses on the person with the most rage. Even in a crowded restaurant, an angry customer will make just about everyone stop and watch. Anger gets noticed.

If your goal is to get on TV and get clicks on social media, some "righteous anger" will do the trick almost every time. I say *almost every time*, because in a crowd of 535 members of Congress, there is more than one person trying to get the media attention each day. So, if your strategy is anger, you can't just be angry; you must be the angriest. You have to say, post, or do the most absurd or insulting thing of the day on Capitol Hill. Some days a little rage will work, but many days you must really turn up your inner angst to out-anger the next angry member or media personality.

Of course, the preferred method to stand out in D.C. is always to be the angriest.

New members of Congress who determine that anger is their breakout specialty will quickly get rewarded when a few people see their rage online and donate a few dollars to their campaign as a tip for the anger show. It gets better when a group of fellow angry members asks them to join in a group yell, also known as a press conference. At the press conference, each of the members tries to say something more outrageous than the last member because everyone knows only one of them will get screen time on TV that day. They must be the most clever or caustic to win the coveted spot on the twenty-four-hour news channel highlights that night. They have a greater chance of being the one on TV if they do the anger drama together. If they aren't picked as the angriest tonight, at least they will be seen standing behind today's champion of anger in the camera shot.

When their angry diatribe at the press conference gets airtime, they are a hometown hero, which encourages them to say something even more raucous the next day. Now instead of waking up each day thinking about solving the problems of the nation, they focus each day on saying the angriest thing of the day so the people at home will think they are "fighting for them." National media is glad to play along with this D.C. swamp anger charade because anger sells, from both sides of the political aisle. Reporters have political biases, but their favorite bias is anger. Anger is the "Siren song" of D.C. It destroys, but it sells.

BACK TO HIGH SCHOOL
ENGLISH LIT CLASS

Quick humanities test: Do you remember the story of the Sirens from Homer's *Odyssey*? Let me refresh your memory from your high school English literature class. The hero Odysseus is on his way home from the Trojan War and is warned when his ship passes by the island of the Sirens that the sailors cannot hear the intoxicating sound of the song of the Sirens and survive. The Sirens appear to be beautiful women, but they are actually monsters trying to sink the ship. Sailors who hear the Sirens are enticed to steer toward the song, which leads to their destruction on the rocks around the island.

Before they sail past the island of the Sirens, Odysseus has his men plug their ears with wax, but he asks them to tie him to the mast of the ship as they row by, so he can hear the song. As they pass by, the Sirens beautifully sing the praises of Odysseus. As he hears the song, he viciously tries to break the ropes holding him and swim toward the Sirens and his certain death. Odysseus hears and sees beauty, but the sailors on the ship, with wax in their ears, only see the monsters as they row past the island on their odyssey home.

In D.C., the angrier and more caustic you are, the more people cheer for you, and the more press attention you get. More social media attention that day means more people donating to your campaign that night, which encourages you to say something even angrier the next day. The cycle continues until you burn out, isolate yourself, or say something so incredibly foolish you lose your dignity, your support, and/or your family. Then the cheering crowd looks for someone else to entice to anger as they gossip about your political demise. Political anger is a poison that kills you and your relationships a little more each day.

Several years ago, I sat in a hearing, having a whispered conversation with the member of Congress sitting next to me as we waited our turn to ask a question of the witnesses. Right before my friend was about to ask his five minutes of questions, he leaned over to me and said, "Watch this. I'm going to get on TV tonight." When he was recognized for his few moments of C-SPAN fame, he proceeded to explode on the witnesses in a rage of anger and accusation. When it was over, he was back to his normal self. It was like watching Bruce Banner tear off his shirt, right next to me, transform into the green Hulk monster for five minutes, and then quietly return to his peaceful self (without a shirt). Sure enough, he was all over cable TV that night. It was a Siren song.

I occasionally have people in the grocery store or in a community meeting at home ask me, "Why don't you yell at people like (fill in the blank here for the latest person in D.C. yelling)?"

I usually answer by asking, "Do you think that their yelling helped pass legislation or solve the problem?" No one has ever said yes to that question. Quite a few people have said, "No, but it makes me feel better to hear someone yelling at the people that I want to yell at." A couple of years ago, someone poked me in the chest and said, "You don't sound as angry as I feel. I am going to vote for someone angrier." All I could think was, *I bet family dinner is fun at their house.*

> No one ever says, "What I really need right now is an angry, bitter person right next to me screaming!"

Maybe you are different from me, but I can't remember a time when I made better decisions when I was angry. In fact, I usually make the worst decisions when I am angry. Most of the emails and text messages that I really want to take back were sent when I was angry. When you are angry, you say the words out loud you shouldn't, align with people that really don't share your values, and hurt the relationships around you that you care about the most. You may think you are better when you are angry, but I bet the people around you would disagree. No one ever says, "What I really need right now is an angry, bitter person right next to me screaming!"

Outrage destroys families, workplaces, and nations. Anger is an addiction, a cancer, a trap. The *Wall Street Journal* ran a story about three recent studies on anger. The key sentence of the story was the synopsis: "Getting angry doesn't just hurt our mental health, it's also damaging to our hearts, brains and gastrointestinal systems, according to doctors and recent research." That sounds terrible, but I bet most people are not shocked by those findings. Most people know their lives are not better when they listen to angry people all day or when they are the angry person all day.

WHY ARE WE SO ANGRY?

I used to be that guy. The one who would have a bad weekend when my football team lost on Saturday. I didn't throw a brick at the TV, but I was just a grumpy guy for hours, sometimes days. Right when I thought I was over it, someone would ask me if I had watched the game and I would start my rant again about the bad ref, the dropped passes, and the terrible play calls. One day it hit me—I'm getting all worked up over the athletic prowess of two dozen twenty-year-old guys I have never met. Why am I so angry about their momentary lack of dexterity? I don't even know them.

Everyone likes to win. We want to see things get better. That may not be a big deal when it is a football team, but it is a huge issue when it's our family, our community, or our country.

When the national debt is spiraling, the border is open, and injustice continues, we get either apathetic, cynical, or angry about the direction of our nation. The apathetic tune out, with the hope that somehow life gets better while they ignore the problems. The cynical reject any proposed idea or leader. The angry try to gripe and complain everyone into compliance. Of course, the anger, cynicism, and apathy grow when we realize that we had griped about the problem yesterday, but nothing changed today; in fact, it's worse, even after all the yelling.

ANGER IS A VALUABLE COMMODITY IN WASHINGTON, D.C.

Angry people like angry people. Angry constituents and donors want to see that their elected officials are angry at the debt, angry at Wall Street, angry at unequal justice, or angry at "them." The best-selling anger, of course, is anger at your own party. When an elected official declares that everyone else in their party is weak and willing to talk to the enemy, but they are righteous and unbending to the swamp, they can raise significant campaign money. There is an old consulting joke that seems to fit our political climate: "If you can't solve the problem, there is still good money to be made by prolonging it." It takes ten minutes to write an angry fundraising email; it takes months of work to solve a problem in the law.

Let me pull back the curtain on modern fundraising and politics.

When you see the online ads or emails hitting your inbox three times a day asking for $10 because they are the only one true to your beliefs in Washington, most of those ads and emails were written by fundraisers who are solely focused on how they can make money off your anger. Most of the time the candidates never even saw the fundraising copy before it went out, and they will never see the comments that you send back. When an email says, "Tell us your opinion," or "Sign the petition," or "We need fifteen more people to give $5," it is all a trick to get you to give money right now because you are angry. No one is reading the petition or passing your opinion on, and the same email saying that just fifteen more people are needed to give $5 probably was sent to 20,000 prospective donors. It's a deception.

Fundraising by fear, anger, and division requires new levels of outrage every day to feed the fundraising machine. Anger may get attention, but trust is still needed to govern. One of the best questions you can ask a campaign is not how much the candidates raised, but how they used your money.

Contributing to a campaign is a noble way to serve the nation and engage in the national debate. We need people who will run for office, volunteer for campaigns, and donate to the cause. Unless we are going to elect only multimillionaires who can fund their own commercials and campaigns, fundraising will remain essential. In my first campaign, many people told me they gave to ministry or nonprofits, but they never gave to politics because it's a "dirty business," which, of course, is true—until good people step in and clean it up.

When a good person runs for an office, or an elected person does something that is worthy of praise, we should encourage their campaign with our words, time, and finances. When people donate to a campaign, they increase the volume of the message of the candidate or elected official. If we want more hopeful, solution-oriented, and calm voices, we must donate our time and money to make those values and ideas louder in public.

Obviously, we are free as Americans to spend our money any way we would like. But if the candidate we donate to encourages more anger for Americans than pride in America, remember you get what you pay for. The way fundraising is conducted will tell you how the candidate will govern or not govern. President Reagan's Eleventh Commandment, "Thou shalt not speak ill of another Republican," is a little old fashioned, but I think we could use a little old fashioned right now.

ANGER IS RISING,
BUT "DON'T WORRY ABOUT IT"

On December 7, 1941, a couple of guys were assigned to man the new portable SCR-270 radar site installed 532 feet above sea level on Opana Hill, on the north side of the island of Oahu, Hawaii. The Opana site had only been in operation for two weeks, and no one really knew the full capabilities of the new technology of radar, yet. Private Lockard and Private Elliot had the predawn shift that ended at 7 am, but they stayed past their assigned time to practice with the new radar. Hawaii was already on high alert because military intelligence had lost track of the Japanese navy over the past few days. Though the United States was not at war, Japan in 1941 was a bellicose empire that needed to be watched.

At 7:02, Private Elliot noted a radar reflection of a massive group of aircraft about 132 miles north of Oahu. He and Private Lockard checked and rechecked their equipment, but it kept showing almost 200 aircraft flying toward them. So Private Lockard called it in to the new Pearl Harbor Intercept Center, where unfortunately most of the staff had gone to breakfast already that Sunday morning. Private McDonald took the call at the center and passed on the frantic information to First Lieutenant Kermit Tyler, who was the officer responsible for activating aircraft to intercept any threat coming at Pearl Harbor. Lieutenant Tyler had been on the job for two days.

Instead of scrambling pilots to intercept the incoming Japanese attack, Lt. Tyler dismissed the radar activity with the now infamous words, "Don't worry about it." He thought the planes were probably the American B-17s flying in from San

Diego arriving early. On December 7, 1941, we had warning; we just did not heed it. The first use of radar in wartime failed to cause people to react in a way that would have saved thousands of lives. By the way, there was a full investigation after the attack, and everyone was exonerated. No one could have reasonably foreseen or understood the significance of the attack coming that day. However, the words "Don't worry about it" still echo.

I understand the national anger; our problems are very real, so the anger is not unjustified. If we want better, we cannot ignore all the anger and just say, "Don't worry about it." We should cheer the people solving the problems and challenge the people who are yelling and cursing for the sake of online fame. A public temper tantrum and belittling everyone trying to fix the problem will not make the situation better.

The growing anger in our culture is a warning for all of us. Public Religion Research Institute found in a survey that nearly a quarter of Americans (23 percent) agree with the statement, "Because things have gotten so far off track, true American patriots may have to resort to violence in order to save our country." That is a stunning one in four people in America who think we may have to have violence to save the country. People who encourage more hatred are not making our nation better; they are providing justification to unstable people to do horrible things and inspiring stable people to commit irrational acts.

Those of us from Oklahoma City understand this fact better than most. On April 19, 1995, a very angry young man, with a deep hatred for an overreaching federal government, determined that he could start a war to save our country. He drove a rented Ryder truck to the front door of the Alfred P. Murrah federal building in Oklahoma City, lit two fuses on the 5,000 pounds of explosives, and walked away. That day, 168 people died in the worst act of domestic terrorism in American history. His irrational and uncontrolled anger shattered the lives of countless people, so he could protest what he saw as an unjust government. We will never forget those who were lost, those who survived, and those who were changed forever.

Thankfully and obviously, most people do not allow their anger at government to spill into violence. However, our anger does affect our own attitude and the people around us, and sometimes it affects an unstable person within our circle of influence. Multiple members of Congress have dramatically changed their pattern of life or home address because of threats to their life or family. Judges face protests and real risks to their life because of their work for justice. We have become a culture that celebrates intimidation instead of respect. Free people should not celebrate intimidation on college campuses, at political events or in any other forum. When a mom or dad screams at an elected official on TV, they should not be surprised when their child screams at a teacher at school. We should be the role model for better instead of bitter if we want a better, not bitter, nation.

Paul wrote to the Ephesians 2,000 years ago, "In your anger do not sin: Do not let the sun go down while you are still angry," A thousand years before the apostle Paul, King David wrote Psalm 37:7-8, "Refrain from anger, and forsake wrath! . . . it tends only to evil." We should not allow our anger to damage our families, our workplaces, our churches, or our nation.

In 1957, Dr. Martin Luther King Jr. said, "Returning hate for hate multiplies hate, adding deeper darkness to a night already devoid of stars. Darkness cannot drive out darkness; only light can do that. Hate cannot drive out hate; only love can do that."

Let me say it simply. We cannot turn down darkness in our culture; we can only turn up light. There is no "dark switch" on the wall when you enter a room because you cannot turn down dark; you can only turn up light. Yelling at what is wrong does not turn down the dark, demonstrating what is good turns up the light. We cannot just do less anger, cynicism, or hatred; we need to do more hope, mentoring, optimism, and solutions.

We cannot turn down darkness in our culture; we can only turn up light.

We could work a lifetime to fight the darkness in our own lives and nation without success, or we could shift our perspective and work to turn up light. Yelling at the dark is simple, but ineffective. Turning up light is harder, but it actually makes a difference. If we want less darkness, we need more light.

9

DO THE RIGHT THING, THE RIGHT WAY

---

*"Nothing so needs reforming
as other people's habits."*

—MARK TWAIN

was a little nervous as I prepared for my first town hall meeting. I had been in the ministry for over two decades and had spoken to thousands of students, but my only previous connection with a congressional town hall was when Cindy and I attended a town hall hosted by our congressman in Central Oklahoma about five years before. At the time, I had no idea the next town hall I attended would have me up front answering questions instead of quietly second-guessing the answers near the back of the room. I had been in office for only three weeks, on that cold day in late January 2011. The team planned a town hall meeting in downtown Oklahoma City to give a face-to-face update of what happened over the last month and gain insight on what people were thinking for the future.

Town hall meetings at the time often included long questions about specific details in the United States Constitution or federal spending. The meetings were typically full, but it was before people brought their cell phones to town halls to record themselves shouting at an elected official so they could be "social media famous." Back in the "old days," people came to townhall meetings just to talk and ask honest questions.

About 45 minutes into the town hall, a very nice lady stood up and started her question with, "You people in Washington" and then proceeded to rage on the problem of everyone serving in D.C. Honestly, I don't remember exactly the rest of her question. I was so shocked being called, "You people in Washington,"

I started laughing. It was a sincere laugh. I wasn't mocking her. It just struck me funny—two months earlier, I was running my campaign as the outsider, as the never-been-in-politics youth pastor, but I was already, "You people in Washington."

By the way, my laughter did not sit well with my very sincere questioner. She went from frustrated to mad in a flash. Of course, I apologized to her and let her know that I was not laughing at her or her question. I was just processing how quickly I had suddenly become "You people." Her anger was not about any vote I had taken; in fact, I remember that she appreciated the way I voted. She was just frustrated that the whole mess was not cleaned up yet. In less than a month, I was the target of rage, instead of the solution for it.

When our frustration is legitimate, what can we do about our anger at the unsolved problems we face as a nation? How can we turn down darkness in our nation and our own lives by turning up some light?

PRINCIPLE ONE:
DO THE RIGHT THING, THE RIGHT WAY

Veterans Day weekend 2023, I flew across the globe to personally thank the hundreds of Thunderbirds, members of the 45th Infantry, Oklahoma National Guard, for their service to our nation in a place few Americans will ever travel, the Horn of Africa. The region is incredibly important to international trade and our national security, but at that moment it was also a hotbed of conflict when the Houthis in Yemen started firing rockets and missiles toward cargo and military ships passing through the narrow strait from the Gulf of Aden into the Red Sea. The temperature had "cooled" to below 100 degrees by November, but we arrived just in time for the beginning of fly season. You cannot imagine the proliferation of flies in Djibouti during the fall. The ground is black from dead flies, and it is impossible to swat away the flies from your face or your food during that season.

Remarkably, not a single soldier complained to me about the flies. Don't misunderstand—they were all ready to be home after almost a year of deployment, but they understood the importance of the mission and kept a positive attitude. As I interacted with several of the Thunderbirds who were engaged in especially tough tasks, but remained focused and upbeat, I shook their hand and passed them one of my personal challenge coins as a thank you. My coin has the phrase, "Right thing, Right way" on the face, along with our national motto, "In God We Trust." I want every person who receives my coin to know my gratitude for their bravery, sacrifice, and service. I also want to celebrate those who do the right thing, the right way.

I hear all over the country, "I want to see someone fighting for me in D.C." That is completely understandable, but we should never be satisfied with leaders who just fight but have no plan to win the fight. There are a million issues to fight for or against, but it's not enough just to fight. Governing means you must win the fight. That takes strategy and tenacity. It takes making new friends of old enemies. Paul challenged the church in Corinth by saying, " . . . I do not run like someone running aimlessly; I do not fight like a boxer beating the air."

When we are angry, we say things that are irrational. I hear conservatives who are angry at FBI leadership say things like, "Abolish the FBI." That sounds like another version of "Defund the police." Some are rightfully angry at the overwhelming flow of illegal immigration across our borders, but they respond by

The ends do not justify the means.

trying to stop even legal immigration. Anger pushes us to policy positions that are irrational because anger makes us irrational.

There is a right thing to do and a right way to do it for every issue. It is not enough to just be right; we must also be right in how we get the job done. The ends do not justify the means. That is the opposite of "There is a right thing to do and a right way to do it." We can be bold and clear, but also full of kindness and truth. Proverbs 3:3-4 says, "Let love and faithfulness never leave you; bind them around your neck, write them on the tablet of your heart. Then you will win favor and a good name in the sight of God and man." Being bold and courageous is essential for leaders; being a jerk is not.

PRINCIPLE TWO: ASK IF-THEN

When you are angry, you want to "jump into the fight, make all things right, and then call it a night." But before I jump into the fight, I try to ask myself, "If I say or do 'this,' then what will happen next?" That simple "if-then" question could save a lot of heartache. Another way to think about if-then is to ask, "If someone were to say or do this to me, then how would I react?"

When I am angry, I want to yell at someone; probably you do, too. Some people just love a little "scrap" every day to get the blood flowing. But every action creates an opposite reaction, that could make the situation even worse long term. There is a simple decision to answer in a moment of anger: Do you want to vent your anger or solve the problem? Usually, you can't do both. Yelling gathers others who love to yell, and then together with fellow yellers, we push away everyone who needs to hear the message we are yelling about. High volume anger can make the situation worse.

In a war, the goal is the forced submission of the enemy, but we are not at war with our fellow countrymen. We are trying to win the hearts and minds of people who disagree, who are not our enemy; they are just wrong on a particular issue. I do not win them over by shouting more loudly, I win them over by engaging and persuading. I fully understand that in a Republic, many times I must get more votes to win the day. But after winning the vote, I should not step on the people who lost. Primarily, because they are made in the image of God and loved by Jesus. I also should not forget there is always another vote coming soon. In the Senate, I often vote in opposition to someone today, but I might need that person's vote next week on a completely different issue. Burning the bridge may feel good, but I might need that bridge next week to pass a different bill.

As a rule, if you want to make friends, then you must be friendly. If you want to win people over to your point of view, you can't belittle them into your camp. The late Senator Johnny Isakson of Georgia, one of the most respected Senators on both sides of the aisle, was famous for saying that he only had "friends and future friends." That is a role model for getting things done.

If you want to fix the problem rather than just explode and create new problems, ask the if-then question.

As a side note, if-then is also a defining question for conservative policy ideas. When you research an issue and ask the foundational question—"If I pass this bill, enact this policy, or make that change, then what will happen?"—you often discover problems on the horizon. At times, a few of my colleagues are so eager to fix "the problem" right now, they are not willing to even discuss what might happen next if the legislation passes. They see the next consequence as another opportunity to pass more legislation to fix the problem that the last legislation created. Before you support a policy idea, it's good to ask the if-then question. Maybe we can talk more about seeing over the horizon with "if-then" at another time; for now, let's get back to anger.

PRINCIPLE THREE: KEEP YOUR PERSPECTIVE

Anger takes away perspective. Anger usually makes a bad situation worse, louder, and more humiliating. Lately, everyone seems to say the same thing about America: "It has never been this bad before," or "We are more divided than ever." Apparently, the Civil War in 1861 or the repetitive assassinations and civil unrest of 1968 were "the good old days." We are not living in the hardest season in American history, but we are living in a tough moment that we should work to make better. There is real division in the nation because we don't all agree, but we should pause and get some rational perspective in this season of change.

Almost two decades ago, when some friends were at the Falls Creek summer camp I directed, they decided to go off grounds and visit one of the nearby drive-through wild animal safari tourist spots. (I know what you're thinking. No, it wasn't "that" tiger safari place in Oklahoma.)

The dad paid the entrance fee and bought his young son, Hunter, two giant cups of food to feed the animals as they drove on the dirt trail through the mock savannah in their tiny rented car. As they rolled down their windows and headed through the Jurassic Park–like gate, they topped the first hill and saw on the expansive plain in front of them a herd of emu running toward their car. They were looking forward to feeding the emu, but they did not realize the emu had a plan for them as well.

In a flash, one of the emus stopped right in front of the car as another one stopped directly behind the car. The remaining emus then started plunging their heads repetitively into the car windows on both sides looking for the familiar cups of food. The giant birds' heads popping in and out like a cuckoo clock were terrifying to young Hunter, but they were even more terrifying to his dad. Their tiny rental car only had one cup holder, which meant Dad had to hold the second cup of food between his legs as he drove. He tried to roll up the windows to keep the emu out, but the car had a safety feature that would automatically roll the window back down every time it hit the emu's neck. They were surrounded and trapped.

Within seconds, a herd of donkeys also joined the emus in the assault on the vehicle. When the first donkey stuck his head through the side window toward Hunter, the little guy freaked out and threw his cup of food up into the air as he crawled into the floorboard screaming over and over, "We are going to die! We are going to die!" Now feed was all over the car, animal heads were everywhere, and absolute pandemonium reigned.

To calm your growing anxiety, Hunter is now a happily married man with a son of his own, who will likely never visit that animal safari park. He did not die that day in the fierce jaws of a donkey. His dad was finally able to navigate around the defensive lineman emu in front of him while avoiding being sacked by the rest of the flock. A little calm, but intense, decision-making got them out.

> *Even if it is the end of the world, I want to go down fighting, not griping.*

Screaming over and over, "We are all going to die!" may rightly characterize your emotion, but it is not going to get us out of the mess in our nation. We need some perspective in our fear and anger.

America is the greatest nation in the world, with the most powerful military in the world and the strongest economy in the world. We have faced and defeated enemies and challenges for over two centuries. None of our current problems is impossible, and they certainly are not bigger than God. Let's pray and get to work. We don't need more people screaming about the donkey head in the window; we need action and perspective.

Even if it is the end of the world, I want to go down fighting, not griping. To say it in a biblical sense, when the master of the house returns, I want to be found faithful, working, and ready, not angry, yelling, or apathetic.

PRINCIPLE FOUR:
DO SOMETHING PRODUCTIVE, ANYTHING

Have you been at an intersection and seen someone honking their horn or yelling at the person in front of them with the broken-down car? (Please tell me, that was not you honking.) Yelling at the guy with the overheated car will not make the situation better for you or for him; what he really needs right now is someone to help him.

Either we can sit there angry, or we can get up and do something about it. When anger gives us a rush of adrenaline, we might as well be productive with that energy. Clean the house, clear the attic, sort your sock drawer, but don't send emails— that is a terrible idea when you are angry. Call a friend who needs help, volunteer in any nonprofit, mow your lawn, then mow a neighbor's lawn, or find any of a million practical ways to make the world better.

Anger can be beneficial when it drives us to action, but it is destructive when we are unproductive. Being angry at government is normal in our culture; we are Americans. We are never satisfied—that is part of what makes us great. Americans see something wrong, it makes us angry, we fix it, and then we get back to our lives. Anger that drives us to justifiable action solves the problem; unproductive anger just leads to more anger and all kinds of evil. When we scream at the TV and write an angry post IN ALL CAPS, the nation is not better.

Remember the Nehemiah principle: When each of us does something, we make a huge difference. Be the person who puts action to your anger and starts working to make your community and country better, if only in a small way. If you need another encouragement to serve people, read over Titus 3 in the Bible; it has a challenge to "do good" three times in one short chapter. In my experience, people who are doing something practical to make the country better are simply less angry.

PRINCIPLE FIVE:
EAT LESS POISON; TAKE MORE VITAMINS

There is an old saying: "Show me your friends and I will show you your future." That is very true with anger. Angry people breed more angry people. In fact, if you are not as angry as them, they will probably push you out of their group. The more you spend time with angry combative people, the more they will pull you into their foul attitude. At best, we leave them each day more depressed and discouraged; at worst, we become like them.

Titus 3:10-11 has a radical challenge: It states that we should "Warn a divisive person once, and then warn them a second time. After that, have nothing to do with them. You may be sure that such people are warped and sinful; they are self-condemned." This is not a requirement to stop loving angry people; it is a warning that divisive people will destroy you and your joyful testimony about God's faithfulness. Their bitter anger will make you forget to be kind, loving, and compassionate. Their attitude will become yours if you keep drinking their poison each day.

Anger is contagious. The more you are exposed to it, the more likely you are to catch it. When the crowd around you is angry, there is a pretty good chance that you will end up angry. But if you live around people with joy, there is a pretty good chance that you will catch their joy. Drink less poison; eat more vitamins.

When we spend hours scrolling through social media, live tuned into twenty-four-hour news, or listen to angry podcasts and talk radio all day, our family and friends feel the effect in our impatience, temper, and emotions. You should limit the intake of poison, so you don't become a conduit of other people's anger.

Do something positive as you turn away from what is dragging you down. Call an old friend who is positive and encouraging. Go on a social media fast for a day or a week and replace that time with positive music. I met a doctor recently who said she requires her young patients to get off social media for a couple of weeks before she even considers prescribing ADHD medications. She told me about the remarkable change she saw in many kids when they dropped social media, even for a week.

Back in Titus 3, Paul wrote, "At one time we too were foolish, disobedient, deceived and enslaved by all kinds of passions and pleasures. We lived in malice and envy, being hated, and hating one another. But when the kindness and love of God our Savior appeared, He saved us, not because of righteous things we had done, but because of His mercy. He saved us through the washing of rebirth and renewal by the Holy Spirit. . . ." We have compassion for angry folks, but we do not want to be like them. We want to show them what happened in our soul when we were forgiven of our past. That was our past; it should not define our present or our future.

> *If you want to be wise, walk with the wise. If you want to be angry, walk with the angry. If you want to be hopeful, walk with the hopeful.*

If you want to be wise, walk with the wise. If you want to be angry, walk with the angry. If you want to be hopeful, walk with the hopeful. To repeat the basic principle of light from the last chapter, if you want to turn down the darkness in your own life, turn up some light in your life by adding friends who do not criticize and belittle people all the time. Add some time with people who pull you up, rather than drag you down. You may find yourself sounding more optimistic after a few days when you figuratively stop drinking angry poison and start taking healthy vitamins.

PRINCIPLE SIX:
DETERMINE WHETHER OUR "RIGHTEOUS ANGER" REALLY IS RIGHTEOUS
(*SPOILER ALERT:* IT'S PROBABLY NOT)

I have heard it a million times at political events, some version of an anger justification that starts with "Jesus flipped the tables on the people selling in the Temple." That, of course, is true. Elisha called out a bear to munch on a bunch of teenagers. Moses drowned Pharaoh's army in the Red Sea. Elijah called down fire on the sacrifice, then killed the false prophets of Baal. Friends will tell me that it is about time for us to call down some fire on the folks in the D.C. swamp to get their attention. The conversation almost always ends with, "God is fine with my anger, because it's righteous anger."

To be clear, God is the only one with righteous anger, because He is the only one righteous. God's justice for our rebellion is always right because He is slow to anger and abounding in love.

There is no question that Jesus flipped the tables on the people selling in the courtyard because they made the Temple a place of profit rather than a House of Prayer (Isaiah 56:7). He was also fulfilling the prophecy from Psalm 69:9, "Zeal for your house will consume me." Jesus did not just yell at injustice each day; He did something about it. He loved people into a better way of life rather than yelling them into submission. He confronted others to help them turn from what is destroying them, their families, and their culture. His motives were always pure; we only wish our motives were always pure.

In Luke 9, James and John wanted to bring fire down on the people who rejected them. Instead, Jesus rebuked His disciples for their impatience with people. Jesus challenged the people to pay their taxes to an unjust Roman government instead of overthrowing it. Jesus served the hungry, diseased, and needy when other people saw them as a burden. Jesus even prayed, "Father forgive them," from the cross. He said crazy things like, "Blessed are the meek, for they will inherit the earth," and "Love your enemies, and pray for those that persecute you." For every example when Jesus bluntly confronted the self-righteous religious leaders, I can show you dozens of examples of Jesus saying things like, "Turn the other cheek." Love, grace, and forgiveness were the primary characteristics of Jesus's teaching, not anger and volume.

Conquering anger doesn't mean just holding it in until you get home. Your family should not be your daily bitterness release valve. If your spouse, your kids, or your parents become the place to vent and gripe about the world, you have made the people who should enjoy being with you the most, less likely to spend time with you. Who wants to spend their evenings and weekends with a person who is mad at the world? Your family needs to hear your heart and life's frustrations, they don't need the daily splash from your cannonball into the deep end of the pool of anger. If you find yourself griping about the government each night after watching TV, watch less TV or get involved in solving the problem together as a family. Your family wants to spend time with the real you, not the angry you who comes out after hours of political commentary and social media.

THE OLD WAY TO HANDLE UNJUST GOVERNMENT LEADERS

There are some other ancient pieces of advice and examples about anger with government leaders from scripture that could be helpful to all of us, including me. The night before Jesus was executed, He prayed in the beautiful Garden of Gethsemane. A crowd of Roman soldiers, Judas (who was betraying Jesus), and some other authorities came to arrest Jesus. As they approached, one of His disciples, named Peter, pulled out a sword and took a swing at the first Roman he could see and proceeded to chop the guy's ear off. I have been angry, but I've never chopped off a guy's ear. (I almost chopped off my own finger once, but that's a different story.) Before a melee started in the garden, Jesus called out Peter's rash anger and then healed the ear of the man who had come to arrest him. That is a different way to handle unjust government for certain.

Later, Peter wrote to the disciples (1 Peter 2): "Submit your-selves for the Lord's sake to every human authority: whether to the emperor, as the supreme authority, or to governors, who are sent by him to punish those who do wrong and to commend those who do right. For it is God's will that by doing good you should silence the ignorant talk of foolish people." I under-stand the truth of this scripture is not trendy in our culture, unfortunately even in church culture, but that doesn't make scripture wrong; it makes us wrong.

Peter wrapped up Chapter 2 in his letter with this description of Jesus: "When they hurled their insults at Him, He did not retaliate; when He suffered, He made no threats. Instead, He entrusted Himself to Him who judges justly. He Himself bore our sins in His body on the cross, so that we might die to sins and live for righteousness; by His wounds you have been healed." That is a radically different way of demonstrating the love of God. It's a lesson Peter watched up close after he angrily chopped a guy's ear off.

This example begs the question: Does that mean people of faith should just allow an unjust government to run over them? Absolutely not. The apostles Paul and Silas in Acts 16 were unjustly arrested, beaten, and put in the stocks. Probably not their best day interacting with government leaders. However, instead of whining and cursing, they prayed, sang songs, and demonstrated the love of God to the people they were around. When God provided an earthquake to open the prison doors, the jailer who had put them in the stocks was the first person to say he wanted to know God like Paul and Silas knew God. If Paul and Silas had spent the night screaming and whining about the injustice of their beating and imprisonment, they would have missed an opportunity for ministry and a huge blessing.

When morning came, the people who had unjustly imprisoned Paul and Silas wanted to release them and conceal their crime of beating Paul, a Roman citizen, without a trial. Paul said, "No way," to their cover-up, and he challenged them to come to the jail face-to-face to make things right. He expected the people in government to follow the law, just like he did.

Paul challenged the local government leaders directly and appropriately. He did not gripe to everyone who could do nothing about the problem; he took the problem directly to the leaders. That is a great example. We sometimes gripe to everyone except the people who could make a difference. Taking our problem to the decision-makers, so they can change and the problem can get fixed, should be the objective. The intent of confrontation with government leaders should be to bring reconciliation and repair.

While I am talking about Paul, I want to point you back again to the remarkable letter he wrote later to a young pastor named Titus, with some revolutionary ideas on handling unjust government leaders. Titus 3 is a worthy read for anyone who needs some solid insight. It's much better than anything I could ever write. Paul wrote to his friend and a fellow pastor: "Remind the people to be subject to rulers and authorities, to be obedient, to be ready to do whatever is good, to slander no one, to be peaceable and considerate, and always to be gentle toward everyone. At one time, we too were foolish, disobedient, deceived and enslaved by all kinds of passions and pleasures. We lived in malice and envy, being hated, and hating one another. But when the kindness and love of God our Savior appeared, He saved us, not because of righteous things we had done, but because of His mercy. He saved us through the washing of rebirth and renewal by the Holy Spirit. . . ."

I can't even count the number of times someone has said to me at a political meeting, "We are going to have to learn to fight like they fight and cheat like they cheat, or we will never win." Every time I hear someone say that, I think of two things: (1) So, you are saying we should give up our morals and principles to show them that our morals and principles are better? And (2) Paul's words in Titus 3, which you read in the paragraph above and I repeat here: "At one time we too were foolish, disobedient, deceived and enslaved by all kinds of passions and pleasures. We lived in malice and envy, being hated, and hating one another. But when the kindness and love of God our Savior appeared, he saved us. . . ."

Not everyone believes that the Bible is true and we should live by its truth. But, for those who say they do believe the Bible, we have a decision to make about how we handle anger at government. We either do anger like the 24-hour news channels and the internet or we do anger like Titus 3. We have to decide which way is right and live it. We have fought for a long time like everyone else fights, and it is only getting worse. Maybe we should learn to fight like Jesus and see if that will make an eternal difference.

10

A VERY PUBLIC CASE STUDY IN D.C. POLITICS AND SOCIAL MEDIA RUMORS . . .

Luke Skywalker: *"You told me Darth Vader betrayed and murdered my father. . . ."*

Obi-Wan Kenobi: *"So, what I told you was true . . . from a certain point of view."*

—*RETURN OF THE JEDI* (1983)

In the fall of 2023, closing the wide-open southern border was my top priority and the number-one issue for most Americans as a record number of people illegally crossed our southern border, month after month. Millions of people flooded the border with little or no criminal vetting, costing billions of dollars, increasing crime, and multiplying frustration across the country. It was chaos. Little did I know at the start of the year how the chaos on our open border would bring chaos to my family as well.

I have no problem with legal immigration. In fact, I celebrate legal immigration. Millions of people have legally come to the United States and made their lives and our nation better. However, I am adamantly opposed to illegal immigration; in fact, I am opposed to any activity that begins with the word "illegal." The rule of law is essential in our nation. Many people coming illegally to our nation are fleeing from nations where the rule of law is not upheld; we should not become like those nations by ignoring our law.

Although most people crossing our southern border illegally are probably trying to find a better job or connect with family who are already illegally living in the United States, it doesn't excuse their illegal behavior. We shouldn't ignore the reality that thousands of people crossing our border each month are connected to violent gangs, are running from the law in their own country, or are connected to known terrorist organizations.

In the mass of people crossing each day, it's impossible to tell who is coming to find work and who is coming to make trouble. Illegal immigration is a serious national security risk that must stop! If you ignore illegal actions, you get more illegal actions.

In 2023, the demographics of people crossing illegally changed dramatically from the previous five years. It was still predominately single young men, but more and more people were illegally entering from outside the western hemisphere. The numbers spiked from China, Russia, Pakistan, India, the Middle East, West Africa, and Eastern Europe. Criminal organizations around the world saw how much easy money the Mexican cartels hauled in by trafficking people, and they wanted a piece of the "travel agent" action. Each person who crossed the border paid their trafficker between $5,000 and $50,000. With numbers as high as 12,000 people a day illegally crossing in December of 2023, you can do the math to calculate how much money was flowing into violent international criminal organizations because of the open southern border policy of the Biden administration.

When international criminal and terrorist organizations started trafficking paying customers from around the world, they discovered they could also move their own people into the United States without being detected. Suddenly, the number of people apprehended at the border who were on our Terror Watchlist jumped by more than 4,000 percent. Who knows how many terrorists got away at the border and have never been caught? More than 70,000 people in 2023 were designated as "Special Interest Aliens," which meant they were a potential national security risk, but we had no credible or actionable information from their home country. Well after their release into the United States, multiple migrants were determined to be members of ISIS or other terrorist-affiliated groups. The nation felt the risk, but Washington was unwilling to fix it because of the complexity of the issue and the political risk to solve it. Washington chose the politically safe route rather than the safety of our country.

The Senate requires sixty votes to debate an issue, which means both Democrats and Republicans must agree to take up a complex issue like border security. To add to the challenge, in 2023, we had a Democrat White House, a Democrat majority by only one vote in the Senate, and a Republican majority by only two votes in the House of Representatives (with a new Speaker). All of them would have to agree to pass the bill for it to become law. That meant people who strongly disagreed on the solutions would have to sit down like grown-ups and figure out how to solve the problem. Congress is known for many things, but sitting down like grown-ups and solving problems is not one of them, especially without presidential leadership. Still, with a clear national security crisis brewing, I had to try.

In May of 2023, the House of Representatives passed a very strong and comprehensive border security bill they called H.R. 2. It was well written, supported by multiple conservative groups, and it covered almost all of the areas of weakness in our out-of-date immigration law. The problem was the politics, rather than the content of the bill. When they passed it, they did not earn a single vote from a Democrat in the House. In fact, they did not even win every Republican vote in the House. The House narrowly passed H.R. 2 and sent it to the Senate. Just like the House, the Senate also did not get a single Democratic vote or even every Republican vote. H.R. 2 was dead on arrival in the Senate, but the problem remained on the open border. In fact, the number of illegal crossings continued to rise throughout 2023, and the national security risk accelerated with that rise.

The Biden White House had multiple tools at their disposal, but they chose not to use those legal tools to enforce the border. Worse than that, they used some of their executive power to open the border more by ending previous enforcements put in place at the border by the Trump administration, and they created new parole authorities out of thin air to encourage more people to come. I challenged the Biden White House to use the laws they already had to enforce the border like President Trump had or even like President Obama. President Biden allowed two and half million people to illegally cross into our country per year; under President Obama and most years under President Trump, it had been around half a million illegal crossings a year.

Clearly, there was more border enforcement President Biden could do, but he didn't want to do it. It was also clear that our weak asylum laws allowed in a half million illegal crossings, even under past presidents who had tried to enforce the law. Congress needed to find a way to compel President Biden to enforce our existing laws and update our weak enforcement law to make the asylum process tougher and faster.

In October of 2023, Republicans in the Senate locked arms and insisted on real American border security. So, Senate Republicans demanded we first secure our own southern border before we provided foreign aid to Ukraine or Israel as they fought against invasion or terrorism. It was a high-stakes idea, but we knew the White House would not close the southern border until they were forced to do it. They had proven over and over that they cared more about the security of other nations than our own.

Since I was the ranking Republican on the Border Management subcommittee on Homeland Security, I was asked by Senate Minority Leader Mitch McConnell to sit down with the lead negotiator from the Democratic side, Senator Chris Murphy, and Senator Krysten Sinema (an independent) to see if we could hammer out a solution. As an unashamedly conservative Republican who is passionate about national security, I spent many long days and nights, on multiple sections of the border, asking the professionals what they needed to stop the daily torrent. Everyone told me that we don't have one big problem with our immigration system—we have hundreds of problems.

We needed to build more wall, change the asylum definition in law, take away the endless court appeals, end catch and release, add more law enforcement agents, put more pressure on countries to take back their migrants, deport more quickly, arrest the people who cross multiple times, end drug trafficking, fix the visa process, and implement countless other changes. Because of the growing national security threat, I was determined to work with anyone who was willing to secure the border, even though I was very aware I would not get everything I wanted. At least we could do something to stop the millions of people illegally streaming across the open border.

The two other Senators thrown into the ring with me to solve this mess were also committed to an outcome. Chris Murphy is a skilled negotiator, a progressive from Connecticut, and the chair of appropriations for Homeland Security. He is smart and knowledgeable about the border issues, but obviously border security is not a pressing issue for most people in his New England state. He understood something needed to be done to stop the chaos at the border, but let's just say a progressive from

New England had completely different ideas about how to solve the border crisis from a conservative from Oklahoma.

Krysten Sinema was a serious and thoughtful Senator from the epicenter border state of Arizona. She was relentlessly focused on getting a resolution because she personally knew the people that needed the border closed. In Arizona, illegal immigration was not a distant concept; it was a daily disaster that needed a solution. I don't know anyone in the Senate, from either party, who didn't respect Krysten as a legislator or negotiator.

I was given one instruction by Mitch McConnell: "Get an outcome." This was not about writing a "messaging bill" that would have a good title but accomplish nothing. My assignment was to negotiate in good faith to get a final bill that would solve as much of the border problem as possible and pass in a divided Democrat-controlled Senate. I was also told that funding for Ukraine, Israel, and Taiwan would ride along with the border bill, but other Senators would negotiate those sections of the bill separately.

We started negotiating in mid-October of 2023 and continued over four months, including most holidays, until early February. We met with each other or with staff all day and often deep into the night. My wife would tell you most days were sixteen to eighteen hours long. We met by video and phone calls every weekend and in person during the week. Most meetings included our remarkably gifted staff, some meetings in the final months of negotiation also included White House staff or Department of Homeland Security staff. Between meetings, I met with my team (Sarah and Jacob were exceptional!), pulled research, made calls to other Senators or border professionals, and crammed down some food on the run. We hashed out major differences in two different small "hideaway" meeting rooms in the Capitol basement, in the formal conference room S219 a few steps from the Senate floor, and then later in our offices. Basically, once the media figured out where we were meeting, we moved to a different place.

The three of us did not agree on much at the start. We did agree we would limit what we shared with the media to make sure we fought out the issues face-to-face, not through the press. We regularly had fifteen to thirty reporters hanging outside our doors trying to get the latest news on the negotiations. Most days, when I walked into the Capitol, the "press gaggle" looked like a five-year-old's soccer game, and I was the ball. The crush of the press trying to pick up every bit of news was understandable since it's so incredibly rare for Congress to have serious conversations about solving border security. From the start in October, the experienced Capitol press corps were skeptical that we could get a final bill passed, because they had seen the border security movie before. In the end, they were right.

When we released the border security final text, within twenty-four hours the U.S. Border Patrol Council reviewed the bill and put out a statement of support saying it would "significantly make things better on the border." They should know—they work the border every day. The *Wall Street Journal* wrote, "By any honest reckoning, this is the most restrictive migrant legislation in decades." The longtime respected Fox News commentator Brit Hume said the bill had been produced by one of the Senate's most conservative members and called it "the strongest border protection bill that I have seen in my time in Washington." However, within forty-eight hours the bill was dead. We filed the bill and prepared for an open amendment process to make multiple improvements to it, but we never got that chance. The bill to close the asylum loophole, create a faster process to deport, stop giving out work permits at the border, double the deportation flights, and increase Border Patrol and ICE agents was painfully and publicly stillborn.

In the months after the bill's failure, I was asked multiple times what I had learned and what had gone wrong. I was also asked whether when I take a drink of water, it shoots out of me on every side, since I was the target of so many shots from every direction during the debate. I can name a dozen things that went wrong, but I can also name a hundred things that went right. I am the first to say that the bill was not perfect; it was far from what I would have written on my own. But in the Senate, sixty people must agree to move an idea, which means both sides must find common ground, or nothing gets done. We forget that fact sometimes in American politics.

There were many reasons to vote for or against the bill. Immigration is one of the most complex and controversial areas of law. Several of the D.C. think tanks and organizations had their own ideas to fix the porous border. In their perspective, any idea or plan that was not theirs was wrong and needed to be attacked. Common-sense ideas for border security, like only allowing asylum requests to happen at a port of entry, were not even seriously considered by Democrats in the negotiations. In Congress, there always seems to be a good reason to vote no. I understand that well, since I have at times also voted no on a few of the agreements hashed out in the Senate.

Many of my colleagues understandably wanted the bill to do more. They wanted the bill to force President Biden to immediately deport everyone who was already here illegally, cut off funding to Ukraine until the border was certifiably closed, or change the legal process for minors so they could be deported immediately. Then-Candidate Trump posted his belief that if we couldn't get everything we wanted in the bill, we shouldn't pass it at all. I absolutely understood his perspective and could see the clear gaps in the bill. However, I wanted to get as much as I could get done right then to stop the chaos and then go back later and fight for more when he hopefully became president.

In hindsight, negotiations took too long, but I don't know how we could have moved more quickly. We worked at the speed of agreement, which takes time for something so divisive. We also didn't have enough committed people in the negotiation to allow more members to have ownership of the final product because we were worried about leaks. Now we know the details leaked anyway and the leaked information was intentionally twisted to stop the negotiation, not to improve the bill.

That leads to my biggest mistake in the negotiation, which was my failure to anticipate the effect of the tsunami of fake news and misinformation coming directly at us even before the bill was released. We knew the issue of border security was hot, but none of us was adequately prepared for the overwhelming quantity of false stories and coordinated attacks. When the almost 200 pages of text were released, the bill was condemned online within minutes as "worse than we thought," "weak," and my personal favorite, "not enough." Some of the groups immediately attacked the bill, after saying the week before that they would need days or weeks to read the bill to fully understand its complexity.

A month before the text of the bill was released, I had a conservative commentator tell me they would "destroy" me if I were to try to solve border security during the election year. Another conservative leader told me they were prepared to bring "the full weight" of their organization down on me when the bill was released to keep it from passing during the presidential election season. When I had millions of social media attacks, I couldn't say I hadn't been warned.

Usually when a bill dies, the Capitol just moves on to the next issue. However, this time the story didn't die. In fact, it wouldn't go away. Democrats wrongly assumed they could blame President Biden's border failure on Republicans, so they brought up the bill endlessly throughout the 2024 campaign. But the American people were smart enough to see the political smoke screen. The chaos at the border was not the fault of Republicans in the Senate or President Trump. It was President Biden's open border policy, and everyone, on both sides of the aisle, knew it.

If you had told me five years ago that my name would be a major part of the Democratic National Convention in the summer of 2024 or that the Democratic Vice Presidential candidate in October of 2024 were going to name-drop me, twice, during the only Vice Presidential debate, I would have told you that you had lost your mind.

You cannot imagine my shock as I sat next to my bride on our couch October 1, 2024 and heard Governor Tim Walz say, "That's why we had the fairest and the toughest bill on immigration that this nation's seen. It was crafted by a conservative senator from Oklahoma, James Lankford. I know him. He's super conservative, but he's a man of principle, wants to get it done." I hadn't seen that one coming.

First, Tim Walz and I have not spoken in more than 10 years. Second, the reason I worked on an illegal immigration bill at all during late 2023 and early 2024 was the fact that Joe Biden and Kamala Harris had refused to use the authority they already had to enforce the border. The White House staff told me bluntly at the start of the negotiations in October of 2023 that they did not want their fingerprints on any border bill.

Tim Walz was right when he called me super conservative. I believe in weird ideas like law and order, capitalism, freedom of religion, the right to bear arms, balancing budgets, American leadership, and a restrained federal government. But, just like many of my conservative role models, I also believe in solving problems, not just talking about them.

It's interesting how short our memory is on this issue. President Trump brought forward a major immigration bill in 2017, which built more border wall, ended the random visa lottery, focused on merit-based employment immigration, and included legalization for DACA recipients. Democratic Senators shot it down. Famously, one Democratic Senator stated during the closed door negotiations on that bill that they had an angel on one shoulder saying this needed to be resolved for the DACA kids, and a demon on the other shoulder saying this is the best political issue they had against Republicans and they had not yet decided which one they were going to listen to. I actually told them, "If you have an angel on one shoulder and a demon on the other, go with the angel every time."

During the Presidential election of 2024, no interviewer asked Kamala Harris why she hadn't supported the House bill to end illegal immigration, H.R. 2. Vice President Harris said over and over during the 2024 campaign that she had "reached out to conservative Senators to work on border security," but no reporter ever asked her when she reached out. The fact is, Vice President Harris never participated in a single second of the four-month negotiation on the border bill. Not one second.

Instead of closing the border, the Biden administration used the failure of the Senate bill as cover to not take any serious executive action on the issue. The politics were useful, but apparently national security was not. The American people didn't buy the line that they were helpless without the bipartisan border bill.

Two months after the bill failed, a young girl was murdered by two men who had recently illegally crossed the border. I can't help but think she would be alive today if President Biden had used the existing authority he already had to close the border or if the border bill had passed and been implemented. Unfortunately, we will never know. I still can't get that family off my mind.

I have been asked countless times whether the bill could come back up for a vote in the future. My answer has always been the same: no, not in its final form. The bill had two sections: one part withheld funding from the Biden administration until they started enforcing the law, and the second part closed a major loophole in the asylum law that had needed to be fixed for decades. Obviously, under a Trump Presidency, there is no need to withhold funds until the President enforces the law. There has never been a doubt that President Trump would enforce our border laws. However, some variation of the second part of the bill will still be needed in the future. Closing that loophole requires a change in the law.

5,000

One number defined the border bill more than any other. It wasn't the 12,000 people a day illegally crossing the border in December of 2023 or the 10 million people crossing in three years. It wasn't the 70,000 Special Interest Aliens who were a national security threat or the hundreds of people crossing on the terror watch list. It wasn't even the multibillion-dollar cost to maintain the chaotic status quo at the southern border or the billion-dollar diversion of FEMA funds to facilitate the entry of more migrants. It was the number 5,000.

Four weeks before the bill text was released, social media exploded with a rumor that the final proposal would allow 5,000 people a day to cross the border illegally. Under their false theory, in a year, the bill would allow 1.8 million people to cross illegally, only slightly lower than the previous year of 2.3 million illegal crossings. The bill was labeled online as the Schumer/ Lankford bill that did nothing. It was textbook false propaganda, a huge lie attached to a tiny fact to give it just enough plausibility to be believed.

The actual truth was that under the new structure, the first person who crossed the southern border each day would have been arrested, quickly screened under a fast new process, and then promptly deported. Every day, all day. It radically changed how rapidly every person who illegally crossed the border would have been processed and turned around. If the border were to be overrun with more people than the staff could handle, defined as 5,000 in a day, then screening would have stopped, and everyone was deported immediately without a screening. So, the first person would have been deported quickly and the

5,000th person would have been deported even more quickly. The number 5,000 was not a minimum number into the country each day; it was an emergency backstop in case we were overrun by a massive caravan of migrants. Zero was always the target number for illegal crossings each day. The bill was designed to make sure we never got close to 5,000 people illegally crossing in a day, but if we had, we at least would have had a way to deport everyone and control our border in case President Biden won re-election.

The bill would have created a new fast-track decision process with limited appeals and a high standard to request asylum, so only the most qualified asylum seeker would pass the test. Currently, 97 percent of the people who request asylum are rejected by a court, but under the Biden administration it took years to get to that determination, and few, if any, were actually deported. The bill moved the standard at the end of the process to the beginning of the process so 97 percent of the people requesting asylum would have been deported immediately after they crossed, instead of waiting years or never. That quickly would have closed the asylum loophole.

Faster deportations would discourage the next person from making a false asylum claim, since no one wants to pay a cartel $5,000–$50,000 to just be deported. We dramatically changed the system so qualification screenings would no longer take a decade to complete; instead it would take days, weeks, or at the most months. Contrary to social media, the bill didn't include any amnesty or give out work permits automatically at the border, it actually would have stopped the distribution of thousands of work permits that the Biden administration gave out every week. It also would have set aside money for wall construction and dedicated additional law enforcement hiring funds for the next administration. It would have been a truly radical change in the way the border was managed. But, of course, that's not what social media said.

I have lost count of the number of people who have asked about the "5,000." Each time I explained how the bill would have quickly deported the very first person who crossed illegally and made sure we would never be overrun again by a caravan of thousands, I watched their facial expression drop. They seemed to understand in that moment what they had been told about the bill was false. Most people then said some version of, "That actually makes sense. I thought the 5,000 number sounded crazy," which, of course, it was.

TRUE TURNAROUNDS FEED ON TRUTH

I have no idea how many places and times I have spoken across my beautiful state of Oklahoma. Each week when I am home from Washington, I travel to multiple locations to hear what people are thinking and give a report on what is happening in the nation's capital. I have been asked every question you can imagine and some you could not. Questions on the federal debt, immigration, energy, national security, foreign policy, and the economy are always high on the list. But I also get questions about aliens (the outer-space kind), whether my red hair is natural, and "chemtrails" (the conspiracy theory that the white lines in the sky are from government planes dropping chemicals on Americans). One of the most common questions I get is, "Where can I get accurate facts without a political slant?" I wish

I had a good answer for that question. People hate fake news; we want the facts.

Everyone feels like they are getting half-truths, or better stated, half-lies, from the stories they read. They just cannot tell which half is true and which half is the lie. Some people just believe nothing is true, except what feeds their own personal bias. Of course, that makes them even more cynical. But who can blame them for being cynical in a time of social media deception and "fluid" meaning for words?

As you read this, no matter what time you are reading this, there are multiple staff and interns posting online in newsrooms, political party workrooms, and think tank communication offices in Washington. They are writing social media posts that they know are false, or are at a minimum deceptive, to encourage people not to trust "the other side." They scan the internet looking for mistakes or funny memes to humiliate people with a different political perspective from the other party or, even better yet, from their own party. For many of them, this is their first "foot-in-the-door" job in Washington and they assume this is just the way news and politics is done. Of course, that's true; it is how news and politics is done in the modern age. The only way it will change is if more Americans quit buying what they are selling and demand people tell them the truth, the whole truth, and nothing but the truth. Truth builds trust in a season when our nation needs to build trust. Trust is the currency of freedom.

> *Everyone feels like they are getting half-truths, or better stated, half-lies, from the stories they read. They just cannot tell which half is true and which half is the lie.*

It's politically in vogue to attack the media, belittle the FBI, second-guess the courts, smear the other party, and then scroll on social media to get the "facts." A Pew Research study found that half of Americans get their news from social media, at least sometimes. Literally, social media is the worst place to get news. Each social media company creates an algorithm to feed the readers the information that will keep them most engaged, not the most informed. Facts are not the priority; eyeballs are the priority.

Crazy false stories proliferate online because we read them and click on their headline, even though they are false. Some podcasts and media companies flex their influence by posting half-truths so they can turn national policies in their direction. They live by the philosophy that the ends justify the means. In a free nation, anyone has the right to post half-truths/half-lies. There is usually more to the story than what is posted.

We have a responsibility, as free people, to have a healthy skepticism of social media, podcasts, headlines, and news stories that seem out of place. We all know in our head that media companies are for-profit companies first, there to make money for their ownership. The goal is not unbiased facts; it's advertising dollars, which come by gaining viewers and online "clicks." The only thing worse than accepting everything we read as factual is having a government agency monitoring all news to make sure it lines up with "their" facts. China demands centralized control over what people view in the news. America is radically different. We ask individual citizens to control themselves as they take in whatever news they choose to view. That's freedom.

Almost all media companies have two different writers for every story. One writer is for the copy of the story, and the other

writer for the headline. They have two entirely different purposes. The writer of the story digs into the facts and puts their
own spin into the details of the story. The headline writer is not
familiar with the facts or details; they have one purpose, write a
headline that makes you click on the story. The headline doesn't
have to match the content of the story, or be true; it just has to
make you click on it. So, when you only read headlines as you
scroll, you really don't get the news.

A speech that you see someone give online could be a deep-
fake, including text, voice, and video. We have quickly moved
from, "I have to see it to believe it," to "I have to be there to
believe it." That reminds me of my favorite quote from Abraham
Lincoln, when he once said, "Don't believe everything you read
on the internet." (I found that quote from President Lincoln on
the internet, so it must be true.)

Propaganda is a threat to any free people if we believe it.
The proliferation of false information should not make you zone
out; it should make you search and research even more to get
the facts. Americans, in every generation, have faced the challenge of fake news and negative politics. In our nation, anyone
can say anything, and it's protected speech, especially political
speech. But we don't have to believe everything that was said
is true; that is also our protected right. We must be discerning
about fact and fiction. We have faced fake news and discerned
our way through it before, and we can again.

The election of 1828, between Andrew Jackson and John
Quincy Adams, was the first election that commonly used the
term "mudslinging." Both candidates threw as much verbal dirt
and mud as possible on the other candidate to see how much
would stick. Twenty-eight years earlier, in the election of 1800,

Thomas Jefferson ran against John Adams. Jefferson had stories run in the papers that Adams was an elitist who wanted to establish a British-style monarchy. Jefferson also placed stories that called Adams a "gross hypocrite" who "behaved neither like a man nor like a woman." Jefferson referred to the Federalist Party of Adams as the "reign of witches."

Adams ran stories about Jefferson that he was irreligious and that if he were elected, "Murder, robbery, rape, adultery and incest will openly be taught and practiced." The president of Yale, an Adams supporter, suggested that if Jefferson were elected President, "We would see our wives and daughters the victims of legal prostitution."

Interestingly, just four years before the chaos and noise of the election of 1800, George Washington, with his skilled ghost writer Alexander Hamilton, challenged the nation not to divide and attack each other. His Farewell Address (which was a letter in the newspapers, not an actual speech) was artful, but the message was clear. In the middle of the letter to the nation he wrote:

> "Let me now take a more comprehensive view and warn
> you in the most solemn manner against the baneful effects
> of the spirit of party generally. This spirit, unfortunately, is
> inseparable from our nature, having its root in the strongest
> passions of the human mind. It exists under different shapes
> in all governments, stifled, controlled, or repressed; but, in
> those of the popular form, it is seen in its greatest rankness,
> and is truly their worst enemy. . . .
>   . . . Without looking forward to an extremity of this kind
> (which nevertheless ought not to be entirely out of sight), the
> common and continual mischiefs of the spirit of party are

sufficient to make it the interest and duty of a wise people to
discourage and restrain it. It serves always to distract the public
councils and enfeeble the public administration. It agitates
the community with ill-founded jealousies and false alarms,
kindles the animosity of one part against another, foments
occasionally riot and insurrection. It opens the door to foreign
influence and corruption, which finds a facilitated access to the
government itself through the channels of party passions."

To paraphrase President Washington's words, if the nation focuses first on political party membership, be prepared for anger, violence, and irrational decisions. Yes, we have differences, often strong differences, of opinion. That is welcome in America and necessary, since people are not always right. But when we stop thinking and start reacting based purely on political party, we are vulnerable to all sorts of passions. Speaking the truth helps, and does not hurt, our political parties and our nation.

On February 27, 2023, after a very contentious national election cycle, I stood on the Senate floor and read President Washington's historic address aloud. Every year, since the Civil War, one Senator stands in the Senate Chamber to read the Farewell Address around Washington's birthday. The reading reminds anyone who dares to listen that we have something very rare in human history and we should protect it. We have a nation that governs itself and can be a beacon of hope for billions of people who want to live free, if we do not destroy the gift handed down to us. You really should take time to read the entire Farewell Address from George Washington; it's a linguistic masterpiece and a prophetic word that is still relevant for our nation.

I had a professor once say to me during my master's studies, "Pursue truth; though it cost you your most precious belief, get truth." At the time, I thought that was the strangest statement. The older I become, the wiser that statement becomes. Why would anyone want to live their life, only to realize at the end that they believed something fake and meaningless? Passionate belief in false information just means you had zeal without knowledge. It reminds me of the wise words in Proverbs 4:7: "The beginning of wisdom is this: Get wisdom. Though it cost all you have, get understanding."

Truth is not a political statement; it is a statement of reality and provability. Truth is not preference; it's true if I like it or not. Truth can be tested and confirmed. Truth can be trusted and stood on in times of crisis. Truth doesn't have to be arrogant; in fact, in Proverbs 3:3 the scripture says, "Do not let kindness and truth leave you; bind them around your neck, Write them on the tablet of your heart." A good leader should speak and live truth, but also partner truth with kindness. Truth is not always pleasant, but it doesn't have to be belligerent.

It drives me crazy when I hear someone say, "That's a true conservative," when someone is loud and angry. Loud is not necessarily true, wise, or conservative. Loud is just loud. If volume determined who was a conservative, every five-year-old in the backyard would be one of the most conservative people in the country. There are few things louder in the world than a group of five-year-olds playing in the yard. If anger were a determinant for a "true conservative," every person who is at the back of a long drive-through line would suddenly expound the principles of conservative thought as they wait.

When something is wrong, we should boldly and clearly call it out. However, conservative principles are not about volume and anger; they are ideas that lift people in every neighborhood and background. Loud doesn't solve poverty, debt, injustice, or health. Volume doesn't necessarily articulate liberty and opportunity for every person; truth and conservative principles do. Just because people sound angry doesn't mean they are conservative, or they are working to solve the problem. They are just loud and angry. There is a difference between being determined and dramatic.

The classic lawyer saying is, "When the facts are on your side, pound the facts. When the law is on your side, pound the law. When neither is on your side, pound the table." Someone screaming at you should make you walk away shaking your head, not walk toward them, as a wise conservative sage.

We are Americans. People have the right to lie, deceive, and yell in the public square. But remember, we also have the right to discern the facts, confront the deception, and promote the truth, no matter where it comes from. Pursue truth; though it cost you your most precious belief, get truth.

11

GRAVITY

"The people who are crazy enough to think they can change the world are the ones who do."

—STEVE JOBS

Are you a roller coaster fan? I mean a rapid-acceleration, 360-loop, corkscrew-turn, high-altitude-drops kind of roller coaster fan. I am absolutely, positively *not*. If you love them, good for you. You can tell me about your favorite ride in some distant, overpriced theme park as I nod and pretend to be interested. Just know, I have no intention of riding it one day.

I gain no joy plummeting 200 feet in an open-air car, sitting behind a 10-year-old throwing up their caramel corn. I also have nothing to prove. I am happily married to an amazing woman who loves me and doesn't judge me (I think) when she and our daughters get on a roller coaster while I wander off to find a snack. I have plenty of adventure in my life.

As I stare at the giant worm of brightly colored twisting metal, all I can think is, roller-coaster designers are truly gravity geniuses. They invite people into an hour-long line to laugh and scream at something that everyone fights against every day— gravity. They turn our daily battle with gravity into fun (for some people).

I have a saying at home when something falls off the counter or drops on the floor: "Gravity stinks." I usually don't say it too loudly because the last thing a person needs to hear after they've dropped something on the floor is my sarcasm. I did say, I "usually" don't say it too loudly though. Sometimes things just pop out at the wrong moment, like "Gravity stinks," which, of course, it does. Gravity is always pulling us down.

Physical gravity is mass and distance. Objects with more mass have more gravity. Objects that are closer have greater gravitational pull. Cultural gravity works the same way, mass and distance. Whatever the majority of people think about an issue and the closer they are in relationship to you, the greater the effect.

Think about this simple gravity picture: One person is standing on the floor, and another person is standing on a chair next to them. Which is easier, pulling the person on the chair down to the floor or pulling the person on the floor up onto the chair? If you understand the most basic rule of gravity, you know pulling down is easy; lifting up takes real power and intention. It's true physically, and it's true in our culture. Pulling down is so much easier than elevating. Destroying is faster than building up. Low standards are much easier than high standards.

CULTURAL MASS

People decide together which opinions and ideas have the greatest "mass." Even in brutal regimes like Iran, China, Venezuela, or Russia, millions of people think and live differently from their autocratic government. Mass can be influenced by government, or a leader in government, but it is not controlled by government. It doesn't mean that the crowd is always right, or the ideas of the majority benefit all people; it's just accepted as "normal." Something has mass just because a bunch of people think it.

In 2024, a song named "Friendly Father," praising the brutal dictator Kim Jong Un, was trending as one of the top views on TikTok. Of course, most Americans had no idea it was a carefully crafted North Korean propaganda song to help control the North Korean population; they just liked the tune they were fed by TikTok. Millions were listening to North Korean propaganda, so it seemed "normal."

George Washington was a historic leader, but he was also a victim of the popular belief that if you have an infection, you should just bleed it out. Bloodletting was the most popular medicinal practice at the time. In 1799, then-retired President Washington became ill and was diagnosed with what was called "quinsy." It is now believed that he had an otolaryngologic emergency known as "acute epiglottitis." In laymans terms, a really bad throat infection. The common treatment of the day was to bleed some to get the infection out. That, of course, we now know is a terrible idea. After multiple rounds of "treatments," President Washington passed away on December 14, 1799, at age sixty-seven. An inauspicious death for such an incredible leader. The practice of bloodletting had weight in its time; thankfully, it doesn't anymore.

But when a cultural trend is destructive to our present or our future, we should not ignore it. We should fight it.

Every trend, attitude, or idea started somewhere and grew into a mass, which pulled even more people into it. Posts that are trending will trend even more when they are trending. A new hairstyle or musician or the latest color of kitchen countertop can be a harmless popular opinion. But when a cultural trend is destructive to our present or our future, we should not ignore it. We should fight it. Just because the decline is typical doesn't mean we should ever accept cultural decline as inevitable, because it is not.

LESS DISTANCE, MORE MASS

There are thousands of examples of cultural slide in our nation, and it's trendy to say that America is doomed and then throw up our hands to quit. When Elvis started gyrating his hips in the 1950s, the world was ending, too. We are fallen humanity. We choose wrong over right all the time, but that does not give us permission to give up on people. Instead, it should challenge us to lean in. Paul wrote to the church in Galatia a simple reminder about days like today: "Let us not become weary in doing good, for at the proper time we will reap a harvest if we do not give up." Galatians 6:9. Culture can shift when determined people push against it.

Fifty years ago, officers told soldiers returning from Vietnam to change out of their uniform before they landed in America so they would not be confronted or spit on at the airport. Thousands of Vietnam vets left the battlefield to return home without any welcome home or thank you. After months or years of battlefield experience, they were told to fly home and blend in. Fast-forward fifty years: Many soldiers in uniform have random strangers pay for their meal at a restaurant, and it's common to express "Thank you" or "Welcome home" to returning vets. How did that happen? Jan Scruggs pushed against gravity.

Jan enlisted in the Army in 1968 after he graduated from high school and was assigned to the 199th Light Infantry Brigade as a mortarman. He served two tours in Vietnam and earned the Purple Heart and three Army Commendation Medals, as well as the "V" device for valor. Jan quietly returned home as a corporal in 1970. The war was still raging in Vietnam and painfully still in his mind and body. He not only carried shrapnel in his body from a Vietnamese mortar round, but he also carried the memory of twelve fellow soldiers he watched die in a horrible explosion while they were unloading a truck full of ammunition.

When Jan returned from Vietnam, he drifted and drank for months before enrolling in American University to get his bachelor's degree, then a master's degree. By 1977, he was married and educated and had a job at the Department of Labor in Washington, but he was still struggling with what he had experienced in Vietnam and what he continued to see in the lives of his fellow veterans. In 1979, Jan and his wife, Becky, went to see the raw Vietnam movie *The Deer Hunter*. That night, he couldn't sleep as he recounted in his mind all the friends who had never come back from Vietnam. He wanted to make sure every person who had lost their life in Vietnam would never be forgotten and that the nation would honor them forever. After a long, sleepless night, early the next morning, Jan told his wife he was going to build a Vietnam memorial.

Two months later, he announced at a local veterans meeting he was starting the Vietnam Veterans Memorial Fund to raise money for a memorial on the National Mall that would have the name of every veteran who had died in Vietnam. There were just a few problems with his plan—he was a twenty-nine-year-old federal government employee with no connections, no money, and no approval for a memorial from Congress. But that didn't stop him from trying. He contacted everyone he knew and worked for the next two months to raise money, but he only raised $144.50 for his idea. His great idea became a joke to many who thought it would never happen.

Instead of giving up, he doubled down. He quit his job to dedicate more time to the effort. His wife worked full-time to provide for both of them as he worked to get America to make things right with Vietnam vets. Multiple people slowly joined Jan's vision and began to help him fundraise and get the word out. The next year, 1980, they convinced Congress to approve a Vietnam memorial, with one caveat: They had to raise all the money to build it. Jan and the expanded group working alongside him accepted the challenge. They raised over $8 million from 275,000 donors in the next two years. It was dedicated on November 13, 1982, on the Mall in Washington. In just over three years, Jan's vision went from dream to reality, and it changed everything about how Americans engaged with Vietnam vets.

The goal of the wall was to help the nation heal. More than 58,000 Americans died fighting in Vietnam from early 1959 through 1975, and for many families the loss was still very tender. The memorial lists every single name of the fallen on the wall in the order of their death. It's designed in the shape of a V with two 246-foot, 8-inch-long shiny black granite walls. The names, etched in stone, ensure the nation remembers each person who gave their life in Vietnam and honors them by perpetually displaying their sacrifice in our nation's capital.

The Vietnam Memorial is now one of the most visited places in the country, with more than five million visitors each year. But it started with a twenty-nine-year-old veteran who could not sleep thinking about his fallen fellow soldiers and a nation that had failed to honor them, so he decided to do something about it. He pushed against gravity.

SOCIETY CAN TURN

In the late 1970s, America was in a bad place. We had an energy crisis, double-digit inflation, and double-digit interest rates. We had American hostages in Iran, a declining military, and terrible foreign relations all over the world. Crime was on the rise, there were riots on college campuses, increased drug use, and we were still recovering from multiple high-profile assassinations a decade before. Not a great season for our nation.

In 1980, something clicked in the heart of Americans. Ronald Reagan defeated President Carter with 489 Electoral College votes, a true landslide when only 270 are needed to win. The preppy generation of the 1980s overtook the hippie generation of the 1970s. Economic activity rose, and interest rates fell. The 1980s brought the personal computer, the cell phone ("the brick"), Pac-Man, and the Space Shuttle.

In 1984, Reagan won an even bigger majority with 525 Electoral College votes. Americans were more optimistic, so they chose optimistic leaders. We awakened together. It can happen.

In 2024, President Trump did what few leaders have ever done in American history, he won the Presidency after he had lost the race four years before. He had a landslide in the Electoral College and he won the popular vote. Against the cultural gravity of 2024, millions of people decided the nation needed a turnaround election.

THE KEY TO MASTERING
GRAVITY IS DISTANCE

One of the greatest mom quotes of all time is, "If all your friends jumped off a cliff, would you jump off as well?" When you are eight years old, of course the answer is yes. It's hard to believe moms even ask that obvious of a question. If all my friends did something, of course I would do it, too, no matter how dumb. They are my friends; they are close to me.

People you spend time with, even through technology, affect you. You trust them because you know them or at least know them enough to trust their ideas. The attitudes, ideas, and habits of a group of people you never interact with on the other side of the earth may be powerful and transformative, but they do not pull you one way or the other because you do not hear them or know them. The voices, morals, and traditions of the people right around you and the people you listen to online affect you significantly because you experience them and trust them. The old saying, "Show me your friends and I will show you your future," is still true. If you want to influence someone for good, you need to spend time with them. You can't be a powerful influence for good if they never hear from you or see you. More distance means less impact. Gravity requires proximity.

Social media influencers, the so-called creator economy, are paid to wear or talk about a product. Companies know the basic principle of trust and relationships in cultural gravity. If a company can find someone who has a million followers who likes their product (even if they are paid to like it), they can influence others to also buy it. Paying people to create content and talk about products on social media is now a quarter-trillion-dollar business.

If you want to gripe about culture, you can do that from a distance. If you want to change it, you must engage up close. Elections often focus on finding people who already think like you and convincing them to vote, which is tough to do. Changing cultural gravity involves finding people who do not think like you and convincing them to change their mind and actions. That is even tougher to do.

I talked to someone recently who told me he no longer hangs out with people who do not vote like him, something that is more and more common in our culture. I responded, "How do you plan to influence or help them think about a different perspective if you never spend time with them?" You can't save America from people who have terrible ideas if you never share with them a better idea.

Self-isolation may be convenient, but it leaves our culture without any challenge. When we pull away, we have demurred to the cultural slide in America and surrendered to the false premise that bad ideas and low morals have more "mass," so they will be the stronger force. I don't believe that's true, and I refuse to bunker down with fellow conservatives and just endure the cultural storm. Common-sense ideas are not left or right; they are American. We should engage with anyone who is willing to hear and consider self-evident truth.

I believe conservative values can help all people rise, in all neighborhoods. However, if people never meet someone who can explain those principles, they will never consider them in their own life. The truth may have mass, but if it has too much distance, it will never make a difference. Griping with friends who think like you will not help the country think differently.

> *Self-isolation may be convenient, but it leaves our culture without any challenge.*

It doesn't matter how self-evident the truth is; if people don't like you or trust you, they will not hear you. When you develop a trusted relationship, you at least have a chance they will hear you when you say obvious facts like: We need all forms of energy to power the country. When you ignore crime, you get more crime. Boys have different anatomy than girls. Exploding federal debt has a consequence. A child sucking her thumb is precious in her mom's arms or in her mom's womb. Work is honorable. Racism devalues all human life. An unbiased free press is essential to a democracy. A strong defense prevents wars. Law enforcement is essential to a safe society. When you value the freedom of faith, you value freedom. Those should be easy principles to pass on, but millions of people will not even hear because no one is close enough to them to have the dialogue.

Our culture needs to see someone who genuinely cares and is living so radically different for good that it draws them toward something better. The more someone suffers the consequences of dumb decisions and ruined relationships, the more they look for another way. Our society needs a pull, a nudge, a challenge to our better angels, a strong influential role model. Don't count out the power of prayer and the purposes of God. Culture can change with a bold clear template of something better.

Almost anyone on a sports team has seen the effect of one good example or attitude on the team. Most people have seen the same thing in their workplace; if everyone is negative, it just takes one determined positive person to start pulling the culture the other way. A friend with a great attitude makes everyone around them better, a great citizen makes a nation better, and a positive family member makes a family better. People want to be better, but they often need an example, a spark, to motivate them. Tag, you're it!

Culture can change with a bold clear template of something better.

In the late 1980s, the State of Texas launched an experiment to reduce roadside litter. The state was spending tens of millions of dollars each year picking up cans, bottles, cigarette butts, and millions of other pieces of trash alongside its highways. Statistically, trash is mostly thrown out of a car or truck window by younger guys, so Texas created a simple slogan to try to change the young male trash culture with a simple phrase, "Don't Mess with Texas." You may recognize that phrase, but you may not have known that it originated from a trademarked anti-litter campaign slogan. After the introduction of the Don't Mess with Texas campaign, litter was reduced dramatically along Texas highways. The positive challenge and example to be better together literally helped clean up a state. Maybe I should have said it "litterally" cleaned up the state. . . .

Many elementary school teachers will seat a good student next to a student who is, let's say, more of a challenge. While that is particularly frustrating to the good student (and usually their parents), it is a legitimate strategy to change the culture of the classroom. Put a solid positive role model next to someone who needs it and allow the forces of good and evil to duke it out.

It's remarkable that we can plainly see that effect in a classroom of kids, but we sometimes fail to consider the same effect could happen in our nation. "We" get better when a single "me" decides to set a better example. Your attitude affects the attitudes of others. Your heart for service encourages other people to serve. Your moral life encourages others to live a moral life as well. You could be that good kid with the positive attitude who could positively affect the people around you if you choose to do it.

SPEAK THE TRUTH IN LOVE

Congress moved into the new Capitol in Washington, D.C., in 1800. Of course, the Capitol was much smaller in 1800 than it is now. On the Senate floor, the oldest desks are from 1819, because in 1814 the Capitol and all its furniture were rudely burned by the British during the War of 1812. It took us five years to move back into the renovated Capitol. (As a random question, why did someone name a war that lasted from 1812 to 1815, the War of 1812?)

In 1907, Senators moved into the Senate Office Building, which is now called the Russell Senate Office Building, just north of the Capitol. Each Senator had an office with a partner desk and an adjoining office for one staff member. Prior to the Senate Office Building, there were no offices for Senators, only their desk on the Senate floor and study space in the Library of Congress. Everyone worked side by side all day long.

Even when Senators had an office of their own in the early twentieth century, they still spent much of their time in the Senate Chamber until the advent of live television broadcasts of all Senate sessions in 1986. (For the record, C-SPAN started broadcasting in the U.S. House in 1979, but the Senate would not allow cameras in until seven years later. Another example of how slowly the Senate moves.)

C-SPAN broadcasts changed everything. Suddenly, staff and Senators could turn on the floor speeches in the background in their office across the street instead of engaging in live floor debate. Good-bye personal interaction on the Senate floor, hello scripted made-for-cable TV drama. But the trade-off was that Americans could watch the floor debate all they wanted.

If you watch much C-SPAN, you already know that most of the time when a Senator speaks, a majority of the chairs behind the historic Senate desks are empty. Only on a rare occasion is there a vote series that brings all the members to the floor for actual debate. During one of those crowded moments on the Senate floor in January of 2022, when we debated voting rights, I decided to push against gravity. I asked a pointed but honest question to start a conversation. I stood at my historic desk, clipped the tiny microphone onto my suit pocket, and gently placed an oversized photo of a 3D sonogram of an infant in their mother's womb onto an easel behind me. Then I asked, "When you look at this photo, what do you see?" Then I paused and waited.

Nearly 100 heads in the room turned toward my desk for a quick glance. I could see multiple Senators quietly moving their lips to say, "A baby." Which, of course, was the right answer. It's impossible to look at a 3D sonogram of a child in the womb at twenty weeks of gestation and not notice the cute nose, tiny fingers, and kicking feet. No one can look at that image and say it's only a random collection of cells or a mass of tissue. It's unmistakably a child. Then I asked everyone, "Will she get the right to vote?"

The question of when life begins and the value of each child has been a moral and legal question for decades. But post-*Dobbs*, the Supreme Court decision that returned the issue of when life begins back to "We the People," the conversation about babies in the womb has become even more political. It's so political, I fear we have stopped even trying to articulate why life is important. Some are afraid to talk about the value of a child in the womb because the conversation can get heated or personal, though it doesn't have to be either. Others struggle to talk about life because they're honestly still trying to make up their own mind about when life begins and the best way to protect vulnerable children and the personal freedom of adults. In the last campaign, hundreds of millions of dollars were spent dividing our nation on this issue. This is an enormous issue of cultural gravity that will take our nation decades to determine our direction.

For those who have demanded a right to abortion for all women, it's a real challenge for them to pause and honestly look at a sonogram of a child sucking her thumb or kicking her feet in the womb as her mother or father sings. The euphemisms "reproductive freedom," "right," and "bodily autonomy" are so much cleaner than the words "baby," "infant," and "innocence." Those who have personally experienced abortion never forget the sounds, smells, and pain of that procedure. For years, they see children around them at a store and wonder if their child would have laughed or cried like that child. Abortion is not an emotionless topic for them.

It is incomprehensibly difficult for anyone to move from being supportive of abortion to being supportive of the right to life for each child. Moving from "choice" to "life" means acknowledging the deaths of millions of children in the womb, which is intolerable to the mind. A shift of that proportion is not fast or simple in the heart of any person. I respect that journey by being respectful in my dialogue to people who do not agree. No one will be moved on the issue of abortion because someone humiliated or belittled them. But I am committed to having that open dialogue. Millions of children, yet unborn, are counting on it.

When the *Dobbs* decision came down from the Supreme Court, overturning the 1973 *Roe* decision, some people thought the issue was settled, but it was only the end of the first quarter. Though the ruling was specifically about a state's ability to limit abortion, the Court made it clear that the moral question about the beginning of life would be returned to the people and their elected representatives. However, before the issue is a legal question, it's a question in the heart of each person.

The Supreme Court allowed our nation to reopen the conversation about the value of each child and decide for ourselves when life begins. That means more engagement with people who are still making up their minds or who are open to an honest conversation about the facts. For those of us who respect the value and potential of every child, we have more relationship work to do.

Laws impact the easy availability of abortion in an area, but each individual decides how they will respect life. If elective abortion is not allowed in a state, a mom can and will drive to another state to have an abortion if there is no one around her to walk with her or give her some hope for the future with her child. Mail-in do-it-yourself abortion pills are now the procedure of choice for most abortions across the country, which puts women hemorrhaging alone at home, struggling with the painful physical and emotional toll of the abortion.

Abortion proponents often compare the chemical abortion drugs to Tylenol, but they are actually far from it. A Senate hearing in 2024 detailed the very real dangers of chemical abortion when a woman died at home after taking the chemical abortion drugs. Tragically, she was not the only one. Abortion pills can cause serious side effects, including severe bleeding, problems with future fertility, and painfully, even the death of the mom. To increase the appearance of safety, the FDA ruled that hospitals and doctors don't need to submit any information about complications from chemical abortion drugs, unless the woman dies. That means, when people "research" problems with the drugs, they will find almost no reports of problems. The FDA has also determined that no doctor visit or doctor consult is required for the abortion drugs, even though there is no way to determine whether a woman has an ectopic pregnancy or whether her pregnancy is within the gestational boundaries of the drug, unless she has an ultrasound. Why can't we all agree that moms and dads who are considering abortion should at least have compassionate access to the facts so they can weigh the consequences of abortion?

Like many families, our life changed dramatically when our home pregnancy test came up positive. We had a child. Suddenly, there were three in our family. Cindy was (and is) an amazing mom. She took prenatal vitamins, ate plates full of spinach, drank an abundance of water, and abstained from her beloved daily coffee. My chocoholic bride even swore off chocolate during pregnancy to give our daughter every opportunity for healthy development. Why? Because we knew our daughter did not become a child at birth; she was already a child in the womb. We already had the responsibility to care for her, even before we could see her.

Every cell in Cindy's body has the same DNA, from her toes to her nose. But at conception, there was suddenly a tiny group of cells in her womb that were different. Those cells kept dividing and multiplying with unique DNA, different from hers and different from mine, because this was a new person with DNA never seen before on earth. Our daughter's eye color, hair color, skin tone, height, and thousands of other physical characteristics were locked in that DNA. In many ways, the only difference between our daughter now and our daughter in the womb is time.

As Cindy could tell you, as our daughter grew in the womb, she was very much alive as she repetitively kicked Cindy's bladder and ribs at the worst possible moments. Never in our pregnancy, not once, did someone deny our daughter's value, her existence, or her status as a child. Every time we told a friend on the phone or a total stranger in a store about our pregnancy, people cheered a new child's life. No one said she was not a child until she was born; everyone acknowledged her life in the womb. The fact of her existence was self-evident and celebrated, from the first moment.

I have often thought about two women walking on the opposite sides of the same street one morning. Both are eighteen weeks pregnant. One of them is headed to her job, where her coworkers are throwing her a small baby shower as she starts setting up a space in her home for the baby on the way. At the party, they talk over finger snacks about baby names, the cost of diapers, and the debilitating fear of installing a car seat wrong. The second woman on that street is headed to an abortion clinic where she will surgically terminate her pregnancy and then head home to go to bed early after an invasive procedure. One is a child being celebrated, and the other is a child being destroyed. One child is considered disposable, and the other is deemed valuable. What is the difference between the two babies?

The first question should always be, "When is a child a child?" and not "When is a child convenient?" All of us who are parents can tell you that a child is never convenient. Is a child valuable in foster care, preschool, and second grade, but not in the womb? Is a newborn child beautiful in the arms of her mom, but simply medical waste seconds before while she is still in the womb?

> *The first question should always be, "When is a child a child?" and not "When is a child convenient?"*

Some people tell me that they are personally pro-life, but they don't want to impose their values on other people. I often hear in their voice the conflict. I am always respectful in our conversation, but amazed that the "value" they don't want to impose on others is a cute baby boy or girl. None of the people I have ever met who are "personally pro-life" thinks that babies should be destroyed outside the womb, but inside the womb remains an option. So, I ask again, "When is a child a child?" At birth? Thirty minutes before birth? At viability (around twenty-one weeks)? When the nervous system is developed and the child can feel pain (around fifteen weeks)? When there is a heartbeat (around six weeks)? At conception, when the child has unique DNA?

There aren't two opinions on abortion; there are multiple opinions. So, instead of not talking about it, why don't we talk about it more, but clearly and compassionately? We can be bold and compassionate at the same time. For years, I have encouraged my Senate colleagues to go to the floor every session to talk about the value of life. We need more truth and more conversation to push against the flippant cultural gravity that makes abortion trendy and social media popular. It's painful, life-ending, and life-altering. We should keep taking about our national and personal values related to parents and children.

GRAVITY FIGHTS BACK

When you fight gravity, gravity fights back. Anyone who has determined that they will start setting an example to turn around a culture has experienced the backlash. It's not pleasant. We call it being "canceled," but the venom is as old as water, dirt, and sin. Two millennia ago, Peter reminded the young Christians what would happen to them when they set an example: "They are surprised that you do not join them in their reckless, wild living, and they heap abuse on you." 1 Peter 4:4.

Nineteenth-century England called William Wilberforce everything in the book or ignored him entirely when he stood against slavery and helped establish the Proclamation Society Against Vice and Immorality, which later became the Society for the Reformation of Manners. He was trying to have less swearing, obscenity, prostitution, gambling, theft, and animal cruelty and more respect for the Lord's Day in England. Sounds like he was fighting cultural gravity. That generation "heaped abuse" on him.

If you determine you will set the example, there will be people around you, some whom you love and know well, who will ridicule you, humiliate you—in short, "heap abuse" on you. When you live in the dark, the last thing you want is the light in your eyes. But if you love patiently and authentically, you will discover that the people who yell at you now will thank you later for the love, respect, and challenge to be better.

Abortion, homelessness, education, debt, poverty, and racism all have legal, moral, and cultural gravity implications. For decades, Americans have talked about all these issues but not reached a conclusion. When we are divided, the worst thing we can do is separate to our corners and talk about the people on the other side of the issue instead of talking to them. The second worst thing we could do is be combative with people who disagree; that drives the cultural wedge even deeper. Some may feel they can earn the applause of their supporters by sarcastically attacking people who disagree. That technique may gain fundraising dollars from activists who already agree, but it will not increase the number of people who support our cause. I have never been convinced by someone screaming in my face. Speaking the truth in love creates more opportunity to win people over to the truth.

The apostle Paul wrote to a young guy he mentored named Timothy with a challenge to affect culture by setting the example. Interestingly, Paul didn't challenge Timothy to set a better example for the immoral culture "out there." Instead, Paul admonished Timothy to ". . . set an example for the believers in speech, in conduct, in love, in faith, and in purity." In other words, challenge the people who know the truth to live the truth they already know. People who know better should live better; then they can influence others for better, which changes cultural gravity for the better.

> *Speaking the truth in love creates more opportunity to win people over to the truth.*

12

NEIGHBORS
AND ENEMIES

---

*"Good night, Westley. Good work. Sleep well.
I'll most likely kill you in the morning."*

—THE DREAD PIRATE ROBERTS IN *THE PRINCESS BRIDE*

Not every neighbor makes it easy to be neighborly.

Several years ago, I was invited to a big celebration at a neighborhood public library. It was a great family event with storybook reading time, crafts, and a big cake. My whole family joined me for this event, which made it even more enjoyable. As we walked in, a small crowd of community leaders gathered at the door to welcome all of us. We shook everyone's hands and moved through the beautiful sunlit entryway into the library.

As we walked into the expansive library, a very excited senior adult lady, who was cutting and serving the cake, quickly moved toward us to say hello. As she approached, it was obvious she wanted to greet us and shake hands, but her hands were covered in blue cake icing. So as she walked toward me, one by one, she licked all her fingers clean. When each finger was free of blue cake icing, but covered in her warm spit, she reached out her right hand for a firm, but moist, handshake. I looked her straight in the eye, shook her hand, and said, "It's very nice to meet you." Then I turned to introduce her to my wife and daughters—who were suddenly nowhere to be found. All three had disappeared into the crowd, without a trace. Poof!

To this day, when my family walks past a table with a cake on it, one of us will stick out our hand for a handshake, and we all four will start laughing. I don't remember her name, but I will never forget the lip-smacking cleanup handshake. She was very sweet, and was obviously a neighbor, but that was a rare occasion when I would have preferred someone not "washing" their hands before a handshake.

As I have said, not every neighbor makes it easy to be neighborly.

We build friendships around common connections like local sports teams, restaurants, or churches. We connect at community parks, feed stores, and workplaces. Neighborhood friendships or grudges can last for years, but we are still neighbors.

This may seem too obvious, but the "we" of "We the People" includes more than just "me." Americans are connected to each other economically, educationally, socially, and in a myriad of other ways. I cannot ignore the reality that the actions of each person affect the strength and status of my community and the nation. To quote John Donne from the seventeenth century: "No man is an island entire of itself." Our actions or our apathy affect us, and they affect others for good or for evil. Simply put, what I do, good or bad, affects my neighbor and my family.

If a person ignores the domestic abuse that they see and hear next door, their apathy clearly affects others. If a gifted person wastes their days and nights gaming, the economy, their family, and their community lose out on the benefit of their genius. If a person sits around liking or disliking funny videos all day on social media, they may give data scientists better ways to target them for advertising, but their family will lose out on their relationship.

In the Old Testament, Leviticus is a book that many people skip over. It is filled with highly specific details on worship for the Hebrews as they left Egyptian captivity more than 3,000 years ago. In the nineteenth of twenty-seven chapters, there is a long list of ancient "dos and don'ts" for the Israelites to help them understand how to live differently from they lived under the pharaohs in Egypt.

The list includes practical things like don't eat meat that is three days old—pretty good advice for a community without refrigeration. When you plant a field, don't harvest grain at the edges of the field; leave it so the poor and travelers can pick the grain on the edges. There is an admonition to not curse at a deaf man or put a stumbling block in front of a blind man; in other words, don't be a jerk because you think it's funny. There are clear commands to not lie, steal, or cheat people in business. Even the cultural requirement to stand up out of respect when someone older walks into the room is in Leviticus 19. But the crown jewel of the chapter is in verse 18, where it says, "Do not seek revenge or bear a grudge against anyone among your people but love your neighbor as yourself. I am the Lord." It's the only place in the Old Testament scripture that the phrase "love your neighbor as yourself" is found. That's still great advice 3,000 years later.

Over a thousand years after the book of Leviticus was written, the writers in the New Testament latched onto the statement from Leviticus 19 and highlighted it over and over. (Apparently, they didn't skip over reading Leviticus.) Paul wrote in Galatians 5:14, "For the entire law is fulfilled in keeping this one command: 'Love your neighbor as yourself.'" Then Paul wrote later in the thirteenth chapter of his letter to the Romans, "The commandments, 'You shall not commit adultery,' 'You shall not murder,' 'You shall not steal,' 'You shall not covet,' and whatever other command there may be, are summed up in this one command: "Love your neighbor as yourself." James even called this simple principle of loving your neighbor as yourself the "royal law" in James 2:8.

Caring for your neighbor is not just a requirement for people of faith; it's a requirement for a thriving community. Many areas of the country don't brag on the scenery in their neighborhood; they brag on the people. When hard times come, great neighbors come, too.

The principle of loving your neighbor is so simple and uncomplicated that it needs no explanation, but it needs a lifetime to learn to implement. It calls us to give our time, instead of just our finances. It moves us to see the people around us as people made in the image of God, even when we disagree. It even causes us to show respect for others in front of our children, so the next generation will learn how to love others from us.

Our relationships with those around us are a barometer for our relationship with God. The apostle John said it pretty bluntly: "Whoever claims to love God yet hates a brother or sister is a liar. For whoever does not love their brother and sister, whom they have seen, cannot love God, whom they have not seen." 1 John 4:20 NIV.

Isolation has become normal in many cities and communities. The streets may be crowded, but people rarely know any of the people around them well. Compassion for your neighbor is occasionally defined as giving to a "GoFundMe" page, not actually engaging with people who need help or friendship. It may be neighborly to give money from a distance, but when people are lonely and needy, they need a neighbor, not just a dollar or a "thumbs up" on their social media page.

Loneliness and a need to connect with a neighbor may be more pronounced in this age of social media, but they are not new. We all need relationships. For the epidemic of isolation to heal, we must take the risk to engage with our neighbors. If

NEIGHBORS AND ENEMIES   207

you want a truly radical idea, I think one of the most significant ways to connect with a neighbor on a deep and personal level is through prayer and honest conversations about the spiritual side of life.

In 1953, President Dwight Eisenhower told Senator Frank Carlson of Kansas, "The White House is the loneliest house I have ever been in." That conversation led to President Eisenhower attending the weekly congressional prayer breakfast with Senator Carlson, which started an annual tradition that has continued every year since 1953.

The National Prayer Breakfast in Washington allows the President, Vice President, Senators, and Representatives to connect once a year for prayer and spiritual challenge. The weekly prayer breakfast in the Senate (and in the House) allows members of Congress to talk honestly about their spiritual journey and pray for each other like neighbors. It's a small, private, non-partisan gathering of the members of the House and Senate, but it's an important gathering.

In 2017, I had the privilege of co-hosting the weekly Senate prayer breakfast and the annual National Prayer Breakfast with my fellow Senator Chris Coons of Delaware. Chris is a friend whom I deeply respect as a leader and Senator. We have frequent honest conversations about our faith, our families, and the future of the country. We are in different political parties and have different perspectives on multiple issues. However, I can honestly call Chris a friend—a friend I think votes wrong on the Senate floor often, but still a friend. Our honest faith conversations have been foundational in that friendship.

When we planned the National Prayer Breakfast, we allocated a block of time to worship together, pray together, and be challenged together. Chris Tomlin, a lifelong friend of mine and one of the greatest worship leaders and songwriters in our generation, led the worship that morning. Gary Haugen, the CEO of the International Justice Mission, challenged us to fight the local corruption that steals opportunity from the poor globally. Then we took time to pray together for President Trump, the Supreme Court, and the Congress. For two hours, we treated each other like neighbors who need God's help and each other's encouragement. There is an old joke you hear occasionally during the weekly Senate prayer breakfast: "It's harder to stab someone in the back in the afternoon after you have prayed with them in the morning. Not impossible, but harder."

If a small group of Senators, who vehemently disagree on many issues, can get together on our own time in the swamp of Washington to pray for each other, anyone could do the same anywhere in our country. We all could identify a group of people at work, at school, or in our neighborhood who would benefit from a friend to pray alongside. I know, I know. Asking other people to pray with you, out loud, is absolutely terrifying for some folks. Trust me—if you want to develop deeper friendships and a better relationship with your neighbors, take the risk to pray together. You need the prayer transformation and they need the prayer encouragement. Plan a regular time when there is a gap in your day to share needs with each other, ask one person to pray, or ask a couple of people to pray. Keep it simple and uncomplicated.

A friend of mine hosts a daily prayer time with the men and women who work near each other on the shop floor (You may call it a factory, plant, or manufacturer—in Oklahoma, it's a shop floor). They work all day long near each other but rarely get time to spend together, especially to pray for each other. They pray for their families, safety at work, and any other need they are willing to share. It has radically changed the environment at their workplace.

Fifteen minutes a week to pray with others for their family, our nation, and the concerns in your community will change you and your neighbors. Every lunchroom, break room, city council chamber, office cubicle, conference room, clubhouse, firehouse, restaurant, front porch, or living room could be a spot for a small group of coworkers, neighbors, or friends to pray together for a few minutes each week. We all need the connection and people praying for us.

A friend of mine, Sean Kouplen, in early 2023 was praying at home early one morning before work and felt he should offer time for his employees to pray for each other and with each other. You would have to know Sean to know how natural that inspiration would be. Sean is the CEO of Regent Bank, based in Tulsa, Oklahoma. He's a leader, a listener, a man of faith, and a black belt in tae kwon do. He is one of "those guys" who always find time to serve and help people. He served as Oklahoma's Secretary of Commerce and Workforce Development, he sits on numerous state and national boards, he has written four books, and he was the head coach of the Oklahoma Little League World Series that achieved global fame because of Isaiah Jarvis's "hug felt around the world." (Watch the video, but bring tissues when you do.)

The executives and the board had been praying together for guidance, but Sean realized that the other employees at the bank didn't have the same opportunity to gather in prayer. So, he sent an email to the employees saying he was starting a prayer team at the bank and if anyone would like to join, they were welcome.

The plan was simple; they could share prayer needs by email and then gather for a few minutes on Wednesday mornings to pray. When anyone would email in a prayer request during the week, everyone on the prayer team would receive it immediately. Sean sent out the email and waited to see what would happen next.

I encourage you to ask two other people to block off a few minutes each week, even if it is by phone, to pray with you.

Thirty staff immediately joined the weekly prayer group. Over the next two years, it amazingly grew to sixty. Not only has it been an incredible relationship connection for the people in the group, but it has also been a blessing to many others as they documented 157 answered prayer requests in the first year.

What Sean created, any person in any workplace could do. Sean founded the 94X faith-in-the-workplace movement (94xmovement.com), which is worth checking out for ideas and inspiration. This is the United States of America. We are free to connect with our neighbors and coworkers to pray for and encourage each other. The future prayer movement near you just needs someone willing to start it.

If you take nothing else from this book other than this one idea, it would be worth it all. I encourage you to ask two other people to block off a few minutes each week, even if it is by phone, to pray with you. Your group may grow in the days ahead, or it may stay the original three. Either way, you will be a part of serving your neighbors, being served by your neighbors, and battling the epidemic of cultural loneliness in ways you could never guess reading this right now.

BUT WHAT ABOUT "THOSE PEOPLE"?

Loving your neighbor is simple, compared with what comes next. What about the people who are not just wrong; they are an evil jerk? I can find a way to get along with neighbors or coworkers when they are polite about our disagreement. It's a different story when people are belligerent, arrogant, self-absorbed, and backstabbing. We don't just disagree; they find ways to highlight our disagreements and humiliate me for their own elevation. Their insecurity drives them to attack everyone around them and demand that others think like them, talk like them, and act like them, because they are the smartest, strongest, and most loved in town—just ask them. If you don't know anyone like that, great. If you want to meet some people like that sometime, I can introduce you to a few.

It really doesn't take much for hate-filled people to express their hate, especially online. Hatred is celebrated in America today on social media. As Arthur Brooks describes in his excellent book *Love Your Enemies,* we have become "a culture of contempt." It's not enough to disagree with people; we now must find a way to diminish them. That, of course, divides our nation even more and leads to more contempt and more enemies.

In modern life, no matter what you do, you will get attacked. No one has zero enemies. I posted on New Year's Day the very controversial message, "Happy New Year!" Mixed in with the likes and well wishes were angry people attacking me and my family and wishing us all sorts of terrible things for the next year. There is an old political joke that says, "Everyone assumes there are some people who don't like you, but only people up for election know exactly how many." Every time there is an election, we get an exact count of the people who don't like us. We also get a pretty good approximation every time we post online.

I think we can agree, Jesus was a radical and lasting leader. His message is still being tested and applied 2,000 years after He said it. On a hillside, just north of the Sea of Galilee, Jesus sat down and confronted a huge crowd of people with a very disruptive truth. He said to them, "I know that you have heard other people say, love your neighbor and hate your enemy, but I say to you, love your enemy and pray for those who persecute you." Matthew 5:43-44.

If we want to make a radical change in culture, we are going to have to do something radical. Hardly anything is more radical than loving your enemy. When Jesus prayed from the cross for the people who were executing him, Luke 23:34, "Father forgive them, for they do not know what they are doing," it's clear that Jesus meant and lived what he said.

It is embarrassing how often I hear some Christian people demand that the elected officials who represent them do and say the most un-Christian things. It's as if their Bible has a little "Ignore these truths if you are an elected official" footnote on the verses that say, "Love your enemy, pray for those who persecute you, let kindness and truth never leave you, or whatever you do, do it all for the glory of God."

If we want to make a radical change in culture, we are going to have to do something radical.

I have several translations of the Bible at my house, and none of them has an asterisk noting which scriptures do not apply once you are elected or when politics is involved. Yet, some people of faith cheer when an elected official speaks and lives counter to their faith and the best long-term interest of the country. We don't get better by celebrating worse.

People of faith have a unique responsibility to demonstrate to the country how to love, forgive, and engage with people of every background. We have been forgiven of much, given much, and loved much; in turn, much is required of us. Jesus boldly confronted the arrogant religious leaders, but He confronted them with the goal of correction, restoration, and reconciliation. No one can say in one moment that children are valuable in the womb, but a person who disagrees with your politics is worthless. Both are valuable. We must decide if we are going to crush people when they are wrong or if we are determined to love and convince people into what is good, beneficial, and right for their lives and our nation.

If it's not right to belittle someone at your workplace, or in your neighborhood, it's not right to belittle someone at mine. As I have said, there aren't two sets of rules for people and politicians. In fact, Peter dropped a huge bomb on the early church when he confronted them by saying if you want to stand out as different people who can direct others to a life with God, then honor those in authority. Then he said, "Live as free people, but do not use your freedom as a cover-up for evil; live as God's slaves. Show proper respect to everyone, love the family of believers, fear God, honor the emperor." 1 Peter 2:16-17.

BUT WHY?

Why should I love my enemy? They clearly do not love me. It's so much more fun to smash your enemy than love them. For people of faith, we believe that God created every person in His image; each person has dignity and worth because of God's fingerprints at creation. However, some people ignore their God-given purpose, like a man who uses fine crystal for a dog dish. Just because they have ignored their purpose doesn't mean I have to ignore their purpose. We should work to reconcile with each enemy. One of the things David enjoyed in Psalm 23 was that God prepared a table for him in the presence of his enemies. They were able to make peace.

Let's clear something up first: Loving your enemy does not mean agreeing with your enemy or loving their actions. They are called an enemy for a reason. I have plenty of political and cultural enemies. They actively work to oppose me and are hostile to my values, my faith, or my freedom. We don't just disagree; we are enemies.

There are also enemies of our nation. Cartels smuggling drugs across the southwest border destroying families and killing my neighbors are the enemy of every American community. Terrorist organizations training and seeking recruits who will carry out mass suicide attacks on American soil are the enemy of every peace-loving person in our nation. A serial sex offender developing child porn and destroying the future for countless children is my enemy and the enemy of any decent society. I do not agree with anything they do, say, or plan. They are an enemy, and I will do everything in my power to make my enemies stop, fail, or disappear.

However, enemies can work out their differences. The United States has a very close relationship with Japan and Germany, though we were at war eighty years ago. Famously, John Adams and Thomas Jefferson were friends until they ran against each other for President in 1800. As I have already mentioned in a previous chapter, that election was personal and brutal. It was over a decade before they reconciled. Even Rocky Balboa and Apollo Creed became friends. (I know it's a movie, but it's a great movie.)

WHEN I DEAL WITH ENEMIES, I TRY TO KEEP A FEW THINGS IN MIND

Protect your family and your heart. When someone hates you and is actively trying to hurt you emotionally or physically, it is tough to think about anything else. It stays in the back of your thoughts constantly. A friend of mine calls this, "Giving your enemy free rent in your mind." If I live feeling bitter toward someone, it will affect my other relationships. I must refuse to give my enemy free rent in my mind, or it will cause me to be distracted at home and with other people. As a caveat, if there is an abusive or violent threat, call in law enforcement. When someone is violent, it's not loving to yourself, your family, or even your enemy to let them get away with it. Pacifying a criminal is not loving.

Most of the time, I cannot change or win over my enemies, nor can I control them. I can only control my reactions. I can pray for them, do the right thing in situations, and ask God to make wrong things right, but even so, their threats remain. In those situations, I remember that I am not the first person to be frustrated by a dangerous or destructive enemy. King David prayed, Psalm 3:7, "Arise, Lord! Deliver me, my God! Strike all my enemies on the jaw; break the teeth of the wicked." That's prayer I can understand. David simply prayed that God would be the judge of his enemy and carry out the consequences. Sometimes we must ask a just God to do what only He can do to make the enemy stop.

I do know that continually stirring up an enemy doesn't make the situation better; it makes it worse. Proverbs 30:33 says, "For as churning cream produces butter, and as twisting the nose produces blood, so stirring up anger produces strife." That's clear. Start with not making a bad situation worse. When someone is attacking me, I can (usually) make my case without being personal in response.

I do what I can to reconcile the problem. Romans 12 says, "If it is possible, as far as it depends on you, live at peace with everyone." Sometimes it's not up to me; sometimes people are determined to be my enemy. When that happens, I give time and distance the opportunity to do their work. Some people will come around in a decade or two; some never will. I am only responsible for how I handle the relationship.

Here is a radical experiment. Who is the person who bugs you? The guy at school, that lady you work near, or the family down the street who just gets under your skin in all the wrong ways? They seem to be mean just because they like being mean. They say stuff you would never say and do stuff you would never do. Not just once, all the time.

Buy them breakfast. I don't mean you go to breakfast together; that could end up with someone committing a felony. It's too soon. If you normally pick up breakfast or lunch on the way to work or school, pick up an extra for them, and bring it to them unexpectedly. No strings attached and no obligation. Pray for them at home, by name, each day for a month. Not a prayer asking God to move them to another continent, but asking God to speak to them and bless them. Find practical ways to show kindness to them intentionally. Your genuine acts of kindness to them will most likely soften their attitude toward you at least to neutral. It may not work, but you will not know until you try.

If you want to know where my crazy idea came from, it was from a guy named Paul about 2,000 years ago. He wrote:

> "Do not repay anyone evil for evil. Be careful to do what is right in the eyes of everyone. If it is possible, as far as it depends on you, live at peace with everyone. Do not take revenge, my dear friends, but leave room for God's wrath, for it is written: 'It is mine to avenge; I will repay,' says the Lord. On the contrary: 'If your enemy is hungry, feed him; if he is thirsty, give him something to drink. In doing this, you will heap burning coals on his head.' Do not be overcome by evil but overcome evil with good." Romans 12:17-21.

There is a quote (this time an actual quote) from Abraham Lincoln for anyone who thinks they have an enemy too strong to conquer. President Lincoln guided our nation through the worst moments of division, by far, in our nation's history. Yet he famously asked, "Do I not destroy my enemies when I make them my friends?" I remember that President Lincoln was later shot by one of the people he wanted to make into a friend, but his ability to calm hatred was a gift for a war-torn country.

There is no way I will share with you who, but I had a long-standing war with another Senator for several years—until we found something we both wanted to work on and resolved at least some of our differences. I broke the ice by asking them for a meeting in their office to talk through an idea. When I showed them some respect, they reciprocated. Don't get me wrong; we still have very strong differences of opinion on important policies that neither of us has any intention of changing. I am still on guard when I am around them. There is no reason to extend trust too soon in the political fishbowl I work in. However, I would now consider them a neighbor whom I have strong disagreements with rather than an enemy that is seeking my destruction. That's a start.

There is an admonition in the New Testament letter to the Galatian church that I find particularly interesting in our modern time of division. Paul wrote, "For the entire law is fulfilled in keeping this one command: 'Love your neighbor as yourself.' If you bite and devour each other, watch out or you will be destroyed by each other." Galatians 5:14-15.

As a nation, we are destroying each other with words and isolation. If we want to turn around a nation at odds, I recall the ancient words of the Greek physician Hippocrates two millennia ago: "For extreme diseases, extreme methods of cure, as to restriction, are most suitable," or as we would say now, "Desperate times call for desperate measures." Out-hating our neighbor has not brought us greater American strength. Let's try something radical: reconciliation and loving our neighbor.

13

WHERE DO YOU EVEN START?

"Let's start at the very beginning,
a very good place to start."

—JULIE ANDREWS SINGING IN RODGERS AND
HAMMERSTEIN'S *THE SOUND OF MUSIC*

In Oklahoma, meteorologists and storm chasers are as much of a household name as professional athletes. Oklahoma news stations host public events where families line up for hours to get an autograph and selfie with their favorite weather forecaster or storm chaser. Weather is one of our favorite sports, and it is full contact. Years ago, I sat next to a man on a plane who was about to retire after decades at the National Weather Service in Alaska. When I asked him what he planned to do in retirement, he said, "I am moving to Oklahoma to watch the storms."

Before you roll your eyes about the severe weather in my beautiful state, I would like to remind you that almost every state in America has tornadoes every year. We just have more than most, but not all. Texas, Kansas, Mississippi and Florida typically have more tornadoes than Oklahoma. *Little-known fact:* Illinois also has about the same number of tornadoes as Oklahoma, ours are just larger. Most people in Oklahoma will never personally experience a tornado in their lifetime, but we all respect tornadoes just the same.

Oklahoma doesn't face two-foot snow blizzards or coastal hurricanes, but we do have mesocyclone supercells. If you don't know what those are, come visit me next May, and I'll show you a few as we stand on the front porch. Our great weather teams will let us know they are coming several days early, so you will have time to get here.

Let me set the scene. When a tornado hits your neighborhood, depending on the strength and path of the funnel, your house may have minor roof damage, or it may be ripped to the studs—you won't know which until it happens. If the tornado is a high-end EF5 tornado, which are thankfully very rare, it could wipe your house off the map entirely. A grinder EF5 can even lift the pavement in front of your house and drop the asphalt as rain a mile or so away. We love our neighbors and the remarkable landscape in Oklahoma; however, every few years some of us experience severe weather in a way most Americans could never fathom. Did I mention that Okies are tough people?

Most Oklahoma tornadoes stay on the ground for seconds and affect only a few feet of red dirt in a field. Occasionally, tornadoes stay on the ground for an hour and travel for miles. On May 24, 2011, one supercell produced a mile-wide EF5 tornado that stayed on the ground for almost two hours, covering sixty-three miles. Two years later, an EF5 tornado at one point picked up two storage tanks, estimated to weigh ten tons each, and then dropped them a half mile away.

In 1999, I held my three-year-old as we sheltered in a bathtub as dozens of tornadoes simultaneously scarred the state and devastated central Oklahoma. The next day, as I helped with the cleanup in Moore, Oklahoma, I paused for a moment and stared at a church building destroyed by an enormous rear tractor tire that had been shot through the structure like a cannon ball. That building was in the middle of town, miles from the nearest farm. No telling how far that 600-pound tractor tire had traveled in the air.

When you arrive at a tornado scene, there is debris and chaos everywhere. Unless you have personally been there, you cannot imagine the emotion of standing in the storm path and seeing downed trees, destroyed homes, and devastated lives for miles. The family members affected by the storm often step out of their storm shelter or safe place, hug each other, and stare in disbelief at all the damage. The most common statement after a storm is, "I am so blessed we survived, but I don't know where to even start to clean up."

Within minutes after the funnel, law enforcement and first responders are on the streets, even if their own house was affected, to determine if anyone needs medical help or rescue from under a collapsed roof. Within the hour, power companies are in the field, working to cut off the power to downed lines and restore electricity to affected neighborhoods. The natural gas, water, sewage, and telecommunication companies assess the damage and quickly call in crews to get things working again. Shelters are established at a local church or community center for people who don't have family or friends close by, and everyone gets a couple of hours of sleep, if they can, before first light tomorrow.

At daybreak, thousands of total strangers show up in affected areas with chain saws, bottled water, trash bags, generators, and pickup trucks full of supplies. Food is delivered as the debris gets hauled to the curb—once you can find the curb. What can be salvaged is hauled in the bed of someone's truck to temporary storage while volunteers walk the fields to pick up photographs, documents, and keepsakes that were scattered by the storm. You cannot imagine the blanket of insulation, tree branches, chunks of wood, and torn shingles covering everything after a tornado. The sparkle of broken glass is overwhelming.

With so much damage, do you know where you begin? Anywhere. Literally, anywhere. Pick a spot and start cleaning. It doesn't matter where you stand; people need help at that spot.

Do something. In all the storms that I have experienced, I have never seen an Oklahoma community just throw up their hands and walk away. Neighbors help their neighbors every time. Some can do more than others, but everyone can do something. The guys with the trucks, heavy equipment, and chain saws are always the heroes. But the person who found a few family photos a half mile away gets just as big of a hug and thank you.

The damage of a tornado does not clean up itself; it takes work from thousands of people. No one can do everything, but everyone can do something. When the storm passes by, grab your gloves and some water because your neighbor needs help. On a recent storm cleanup, I ran into some guys from fifty miles away who had brought some lumber and shingles because they knew when they arrived, some houses would need emergency roof repair. Just neighbors helping total strangers.

Unless you have personally experienced the shock of a major storm, you cannot understand the feeling of hopelessness as you scan your suddenly former home. However, when a few people start cleaning up the mess around you, emotions change. When the tree limbs are off the house, when the hole in the roof has been patched, or when the neighbor's car has been pulled out of your living room, you experience a feeling of hope that things can get better. The house is still a disaster, and there is a very long road to recovery ahead, but something just got a little better. If something got better, maybe something else could get better. Maybe, just maybe, in the distant future, we will recover. We just need someone to do something to make things a little better.

As we survey the disaster of our modern culture, it's easy to focus on the debris and not the recovery. The devastation of addiction, homelessness, anger, mental illness, anxiety, debt, broken families, abortion, domestic violence, and racism mar the lives and faces of friends and neighbors around us. It feels like it's getting worse each day. Our communities need someone to do something to help clean up, even a little, so people can have hope things can improve. But where do you start with so much pain? Anywhere. Literally, anywhere.

> *God put that issue on your heart for a reason.*

Is there someone you know who is overwhelmed and needs help? Do you find yourself consistently griping about a certain neighborhood crime issue, drug problem, family challenge, or national crisis? No one really has enough time to volunteer or to run a political race. But when you see who is running for that city council race or school board, are you going to complain about "the quality of the candidates" when, in the back of your mind, you know that you should have engaged? God put that issue on your heart for a reason.

As a refresher from a few chapters ago, remember Nehemiah was overwhelmed with the needs in Jerusalem, while his brother was uninterested. One of them asked God for help to change the status quo; the other just walked away and said, "It stinks to be them." When you see the pain around you, remember the first principle in Nehemiah: If you want to change the world, pray, and then get to work.

START WHERE YOU STAND

Years ago, I watched the news with the rest of the nation and saw another racially motivated shooting in America. This one hit me differently from others before. I don't know why; it just did. It caused me to pause and ask God whether He was laying something on my heart for a reason. As I grieved, I started praying about the direction of the nation. Americans want a new law, resolution, or vote in Congress to solve racial and cultural problems, but our greatest challenges cannot be solved entirely by a vote; they are heart issues and family issues, more than legislative issues.

Racial reconciliation has been unfinished work in our nation for centuries, but it does not mean that we should ignore the problem because it is bigger than any person or generation. America has made incredible racial progress, but there is clearly more work to be done. I don't have the ability to heal every heart of the evil of racial hatred, intolerance, and injustice, but I can, and should, do something. The next week, I shared with my staff that I was praying about the issue and was determined we were not going to sit around and do nothing.

For several weeks, I asked multiple people, of all races, a simple question: "Has your family ever had a family of another race in your home for dinner?" I was surprised that almost no one told me yes, from any race. Most people responded to me, "I have friends of other races." I would gently prod them and say, "That's not what I asked. I asked if you have ever had a family of another race in your home for a meal." I had many non-responses and a few, "Let me think about it." The worst response I had was someone who asked, "What would we talk about if they came over for a meal?" After I recovered from my shock, I think I said something like, "How about the weather, football, and how your kids are doing, like a normal conversation?"

Race is a heart issue, and sometimes it's a toxic generational family issue. We still have communities across America where we live segregated and isolated. We interact with people during school, work, and eating out, but friendships and families are still separated. Kids grow up with people of other races at their school, but those families are never in their home. It may not be intentional, but it leaves an impression on a child. To break that generational racial separation, kids need to see their parents interacting with families of other races to understand how wonderfully normal that relationship should be in our nation.

After several weeks of prayer and conversations with random people, I came back to my team with a simple idea: Solution Sundays. One family inviting another family of a different race to their home for a meal. No dues, no website, no formal list of questions; just a simple invitation to a deeper friendship and an opportunity to break a generational chain over a meal in your home. Sunday is a slower day for most Americans, so it's a perfect day to invite someone over for a meal. If Sundays don't work for your schedule, pick any day you would like; just invite a family of another race to your home for a meal.

The concept of Solution Sundays forces each person to think through whom they would invite to their home. They must consider whether they have a relationship deep enough with a person of another race that it wouldn't be awkward to invite that family over for a meal. When someone realizes they don't know anyone they could invite over, then they realize they don't have friends of another race; they just have *acquaintances* of another race. There is a huge difference between being friendly and having friends.

Step one to solving the heart issue of race in America is developing real cross-racial friendships. We will never get all the issues on the table about race until we get our feet under the same table. It's remarkable how many good things in our life and friendships happen around food and the dinner table. Why would this be any different? There is no substitute for walking across the threshold of someone's home to deepen relationships, no matter the background. By the way, the absolute "no-no" of Solution Sundays is organized multiracial mass meals at a restaurant or public location. If you are "assigned" to sit with another family, or if two churches combine for a meal in the church basement, you are being friendly, not developing friends.

My office partnered with the office of Senator Tim Scott of South Carolina to share the idea publicly. At first, the idea was mocked as too simple and too small. But each time someone challenged the simplistic concept of Solution Sundays, I just asked them the question, "Has your family ever had a family of another race in your home for a meal?" You can guess what their answer was most of the time. If you think this idea is too simple, may I ask you the same question? The threshold of our homes is a racial barrier that needs to come down for the sake of our children and the future of the country. Our kids need to see normal conversation happening around the dinner table with people of all races.

After we launched Solution Sundays, I discovered someone else in Oklahoma who had a similar idea and was also pulling people together for a meal—Pastor Clarence Hill. When Cindy and I met Clarence and his bride, Alicia, we found lifelong friends immediately. They invited us over for a meal at their house, where we discovered they have a tradition of allowing the kids to pick a song that everyone sings before the start of every dinner. For the record, when I was growing up, it was against the rules to sing at the table. At their house, everyone sings at the table. We had the best time over dinner, and we continue to admire their passion and ideas for racial unity. If you are interested in learning more about building friendships across cultural divides, look up Dr. Clarence Hill's "Dream Clock" concept. He has spent years thinking through the steps to healing and restoration (clarencehilljr.com). He is currently challenging people to host a "neighbor's party" to push back on the isolation that is devastating our culture. Clarence is full of great ideas and application.

I wish I could tell you that in the years following our launch of Solution Sundays, racial peace and harmony broke out across America and resolved all differences. Obviously, that's not true. But many of the families that took the challenge later contacted me to say that something changed in them and in their family. They admitted that they had a blind spot, an unintentional barrier in their relationships.

I share the story of Solution Sundays with you for two reasons. First, I still challenge people of all races to help make us a more perfect union and to demonstrate the love of God to every person of every background over dinner in your home. Second, I wanted you to know that doing something doesn't mean solving the whole issue. Most of the problems we face in society are so large and complicated that they will take literally generations to resolve, but we should still engage. The Great Wall of China took 2,500 years to build. Notre Dame Cathedral in Paris took almost 200 years to build, the first time. Our national debt is so large, it will take more than a generation to get us back on track. Some things take a long time and a whole lot of people, but they don't get finished if we don't get started.

Two of the greatest advocates for women's suffrage, Elizabeth Cady Stanton and Susan B. Anthony, died before the Nineteenth Amendment, giving women the right to vote, was ratified in

Most of the problems we face in society are so large and complicated that they will take literally generations to resolve, but we should still engage.

1920. Both were outspoken advocates and passionate leaders, but they worked their whole life and never saw the result of their work. Both faced incredible persecution and violence. But without their speeches, advocacy, and organization, women would not have finally achieved the right to vote in 1920. They were leaders in their generation for good, though it was another generation who finished the task.

Earlier I mentioned William Wilberforce, who worked for decades to end the slave trade in England. He debated and challenged slavery as a member of Parliament and as a Christian. He once said, "God Almighty has set before me two great objects, the suppression of the Slave Trade and the Reformation of Manners." Those were two huge tasks in nineteenth-century England, ending slavery and bringing a return to morals and manners in society. After working his whole life, facing ridicule, isolation, and chronic illness, William Wilberforce died one month before slavery was finally abolished in England. As for the second of his "great objects," the British having better manners, I think I will allow others to be the judge of that great object. There is no question that Wilberforce made an enormous change in society and certainly in the slave trade, though neither task was finished when he died.

In Hebrews 11, there is a long list of remarkable leaders in the Old Testament, and then the comment, "These were all commended for their faith, yet none of them received what had been promised." In other words, they all had tremendous faith, made a huge difference, and had historic impact, but they died before seeing everything to completion. It is admirable to work on a God-sized problem that is so large, so generational, and so challenging that you realize you cannot solve it alone and you will never get the credit for solving it, because you were one player in a very large orchestra. That fact, though, should not prevent you from praying for some days and then getting to work. Doing something is so much better than doing nothing.

14

JOY IN THE JOURNEY

"Joyful, joyful, we adore Thee
God of glory, Lord of love
Hearts unfold like flow'rs before Thee
Op'ning to the Sun above
Melt the clouds of sin and sadness
Drive the dark of doubt away
Giver of immortal gladness
Fill us with the light of day"

—HENRY VAN DYKE (1907)

I have a lifelong friend who checks on me often. He never fails to remind me each time we text that I should have "joy in the battle." I must admit, I ignored his challenge for years. His "Joy in the Battle" signature line at the end of his text read like a "Sincerely" I could ignore. After more than a decade, his persistence finally got to me. I was completely missing the joy of the journey each day with God. I am focused, driven, and forgetful of past accomplishments. I stink at celebrating a win. It's a weakness that I can only overcome with the discipline to reflect on God's goodness, regardless of my circumstances.

We have become a nation that is eager to gripe, pessimistic, and willing to believe all bad news. In short, we have lost the joy and optimism that things will ever get better. When we live afraid of tomorrow, we are usually discontent with today.

The real question that determines joy in the journey is simple: "Is God faithful today like He was yesterday?" If He is, then we can have an optimistic hope and an unexplainable peace that none of the problems we face are bigger than God. The world is not on our shoulders, it's on His.

Joy is not a result of happy situations around you; it grows out of the knowledge that a faithful God will be there, especially in the storm. When you remember that God has been faithful in the past, you can remember and be confident that God will be there in the next hard moment as well.

The Bible has a wide diversity of genres of literature, poetry, history, correspondence, prophecy, and laments. Most of those are very familiar to modern readers, except the laments. A lament is just what it sounds like, a poetic complaint about the current situation in life. We certainly know how to complain, but we usually don't do it in poetic style (at least I don't).

When we live afraid of tomorrow, we are usually discontent with today.

The Bible has a painful, but beautiful, complaint, appropriately called, "Lamentations." You would think that a lament would be a strange place to look for joy and faithfulness. However, in the middle of the five chapters of the Book of Lamentations, one of the most quoted verses of hope stands out in all the words of pain written 2,600 years ago as the city of Jerusalem was being destroyed by the Babylonian conquerors, and the people were being dragged into captivity in chains. In the literal center of incomprehensible suffering, the lament included the words "Because of the Lord's great love we are not consumed, for his compassions never fail. They are new every morning; great is your faithfulness. I say to myself, 'The Lord is my portion; therefore I will wait for Him.' The Lord is good to those whose hope is in Him, to the one who seeks Him; it is good to wait quietly for the salvation of the Lord." Lamentations 3:22-26.

The words in Lamentations 3 don't ignore the reality of the pain and struggle, but they also don't ignore the reality of God's compassion and faithfulness. The writer of that ancient lament was looking for God to come through, instead of looking for the next horrible thing to occur. Even his sorrowful lament had a hopeful statement of faith. He had joy in a painful journey because he chose to look for a faithful and loving God in the worst of situations.

Almost every movie plot has a crucible moment when the hero must endure real pain and suffering before the victory. However, in real life, we wonder what will happen this time. The storm and brokenness of life and relationships give God an opportunity to show His faithfulness again. God displays His power when He forgives, repairs, and redeems.

Several years ago, I was introduced to the artist Chris McGahn, owner of the Bella Forte glass studio in Oklahoma City. He blows glass into remarkable art that you must see and touch to fully appreciate. In 2009 Chris, along with his son Micah, created a work they call *Redento Raffinato*, Italian for "redeemed elegance." The blown glass vase is shaped like a tall flame with incredible color and movement. But this art has a unique journey; it's formed out of broken glass that has been reblown. I have watched the process of creating the art, and it's truly breathtaking. As is true for any great art, the *Redento Raffinato* has deep and significant meaning; what was once broken has been made into something beautiful. It has been redeemed. It's an elegant picture of what Jesus does in our lives. He picks up the broken pieces and remakes us into something worthy. He redeems us.

I have one of Chris's signature pieces in my office in Washington. It stands silently in the corner as a quiet reminder that God specializes in taking what is broken and making something beautiful. Every time someone is in my office complaining that our country is too broken, too angry, too divided, or too in debt, I point to the majestic vase in the corner and tell them that I believe in a God who redeems broken things.

In scripture, the Promised Land is described as a land flowing with milk and honey. That sounds sticky, but also wonderful. Until you realize that a land flowing with milk and honey must have also had lots of cow poop and bees. You can't have honey without bees, and you don't get milk without some poop; that's self-evident. The Promised Land would not have sounded as great if it had been described as the land full of cow poop and bees (especially to my daughter Jordan). Those who walk in joy recognize the faithfulness of God and see the milk and honey more than they see the cow poop and bees. Both are there, but only one is the focus.

In the greatest nation in the world with the greatest opportunity in the history of the world, I hear way too many people spending their days focused on the challenges. It's a choice to remember God's faithfulness and His willingness to redeem what's broken, then walk with joy in our journey and task. Being bitter about what we don't have is not better than being joyful about what we do have. That's not naïve, it's a commitment to joyfully doing something about what's wrong and believing that God still cares about our lives and our nation.

PERSPECTIVE

Political junkies live and breathe the sport of politics and love to talk about how the next race is the most important thing ever. Without a doubt, elections and the politics around them affect our nation's future and the direction of our present. People should vote, share their ideas, and do something to help our nation be better. But if politics is everything to you, you need some perspective.

Primary election night 2022 was a hard night for my family. You would think it was a joyous celebration from the photos. I won the primary election with the highest percentage and highest number of votes I had ever received in a primary election. It was a huge victory. The state saw my family on stage during the election night watch party smiling, and thanking the many people who had invested their time and finances in our campaign to solve the challenges we face as a nation. No one in the crowded watch party that night knew we were in the middle of a final exam on perspective.

A year earlier, my mom's Parkinson's disease took a turn. After more than a decade of managing that terrible disease, the medication was no longer working the same. Her body and mind were no longer aligned. Our family decided together it was time to step up her care, so she moved into a memory care unit very close to our house to receive twenty-four-hour attention. Mom had her same great attitude and outlook, but she was fading away from us.

The week before the primary election, we had a small family birthday party for my mom with cake and ice cream. She was smiling and enjoying the moment. Two days later, she was in Mercy Hospital, semi-awake only a few minutes a day. She was initially diagnosed with a powerful, but treatable, infection, but even after a round of IV antibiotics, she could not wake up. We canceled all campaign events leading up to election night to be with her at this vulnerable moment.

On the day of the primary election, I took some media interviews, traveled to a few places, did the watch party, and then headed back to the hospital for the night. Her infection was getting better, but she still was not conscious. A scan the next morning revealed she had quietly suffered dozens of strokes. We were now dealing with something much more serious. We sat with her for the next few days to watch the remarkable staff at the hospital live up to their name, Mercy. A week after the election, I watched Mom take her final breath early on the morning of July 4th, her Independence Day from Parkinson's.

As we walked out of the hospital at sunrise, I got a text message from a friend who asked if I would be at the Edmond LibertyFest Parade that morning. All I could text back was, "Not this year." I wasn't thinking about the primary election victory or the political challenges yet to come; I was thinking about my mom and the fragility of life. It was perspective.

It seems like we would keep up with something as important as perspective. But we seem to lose it as much as keys, sunglasses, and umbrellas. We have it for a season, and then we lose it again. Perspective is what keeps you focused on what is important in life and what is only interesting or frustrating for a moment. When we are out of perspective, we allow our minds to be consumed with the trivial and passing instead of the vital or eternal.

When I travel around my state, I hear many ideas, stories, and concerns, but my favorite thing to hear is when someone says, "I remember when you were the director of Falls Creek." That simple statement almost always starts a deep conversation about life change, faith, and personal growth. Falls Creek is the largest summer camp in America. It's where teenagers in Oklahoma go to get away from their parents for a week during the summer, but also find a new perspective on faith and life.

Years later, I still hear the stories of how a week at camp changed someone's life perspective forever.

A few weeks before my predecessor in the Senate, Dr. Tom Coburn, passed away, I stopped to visit with him at his home in Tulsa. Dr. Coburn was a living legend in the Senate and a passionate voice for getting our nation out of debt. In his final days, his mind was still sharp, but his body was dealing with the deepening effects of cancer. While I was there, he gave me his copy of the classic book on keeping the main thing the main thing in faith, *The Great Omission,* by Dallas Willard. It was marked up and highlighted on almost every page. It had obviously been read multiple times. Page after page of underlines, stars, and highlights gave a picture of Dr. Coburn's priority. He was the one Washington called "Dr. No" and the Senator most people would remember for his work on our national debt. But Dr. Coburn was also a man who kept his focus on loving God, loving his family, and helping people know God. He kept his faith and family perspective.

I pray that this book has given you a moment to reflect on your own priorities and perspective. There are things that are important for a moment and things that are important for an eternity. We should remember which ones are which. We should be the people whom God created us to be and do the things He created us to do, with joy and calling. The apostle Paul wrote in the letter to the Ephesians that "we are God's handiwork, created in Christ Jesus to do good works. . . ." That means we were each created by God for a purpose He prepared for us to do.

Since we're all built by God for a purpose, maybe our days would be more joyful if we were to find that purpose and live it. Our soul and our nation are longing for it.

ABOUT THE AUTHOR

JAMES LANKFORD is a husband, a dad of two gifted daughters, a former youth pastor, and a United States Senator for the remarkable people of Oklahoma. James is a passionate and proud conservative who serves in multiple key roles in Congress for national security and economic opportunity. He is driven by his faith in Jesus, a love for his family, and his hope for our nation.  He has appeared on every major network and in most major publications (and a few you have never heard of). Whether media outlets agree or disagree, James is committed to challenging all of us to live our values and planting truth in the rich soil of our nation's heritage to watch it grow.

Visit the author at JamesLankford.com.

Learn more about Senator Lankford at Lankford.Senate.gov.